Memoir of a Pilgrim Preacher: A True Adventure in Faith

Pilgrim Preacher

Published by Pilgrim Preacher, 2023.

MEMOIR OF A PILGRIM PREACHER: A TRUE ADVENTURE IN FAITH

First edition. November 17, 2023.

Copyright © 2023 Pilgrim Preacher.

ISBN: 979-8223271758

Written by Pilgrim Preacher.

Table of Contents

Dedicated to the puritan families who supported me in my pilgrimage.

First Edition printed by Blurb 2014.

Second Edition published in online bookstores 2021.

Third Edition published in online bookstores 2023.

Book Notes: A Bold type beginning a paragraph indicates a new journal entry.

Check out the glossary section for abbreviations and explanations.

Memoir of a Pilgrim Preacher is the story of The Pilgrim Band Ministry – who founded it, how and why, and the adventures along the way. It is a story of the highs and lows of human experience, the search for identity, the struggle for survival, and the efforts employed to preserve the nation in righteousness. Come along for this journey!

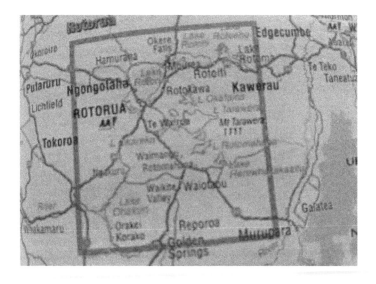

Chapter One: The Early Years

This chapter covers the period of The Pilgrim Preachers youth and first five years in the BBC Movement. The sapling takes root in the first eighteen years of youth, in the encounter with the living Christ and the consequent innocent beginning in the church. Come with me in this journey...

I was born and raised in a small farming community one hours drive south of Rotorua City. I had a pleasant childhood which I would not swap for anything. I was privileged to grow up surrounded by nature – glorious nature. In this environment, my two older brothers, two younger sisters and I had no limit in our exploration of our world; no boundaries as our imaginations ran wild in our zest for life.

Yes, we worked too: when we came home from school and on weekends, we would toil side by side on the farm. This fitted each of us with a work ethic that would benefit us in the coming years. We were an industrious family and well-established in the community.

My favorite pastimes on the farm were keeping poultry, writing short stories, and penning lyrics. From my earliest days, I enjoyed a vivid imagination and the blessing of being a channel for inspiration. It was my intention to be an author.

The farm was well situated, with a creek running through it and a river running along the rear boundary. This afforded us abundant opportunities for hunting and fishing. The valley was of extremes weather-wise – with deep white frosts in the winter and dusty droughts in the summer. It was, as I said, a childhood surrounded by the wonders of the natural world. I was a natural man, and unbeknown to my awareness for the first eighteen years of my life, I was a natural man in the spiritual sense too. Let me now begin relating the events that led up to my true conversion and subsequent adventures.

My family was religious, attending on occasion the local Presbyterian Church or the not-so-local Dutch Reformed Church in the large town of Tokoroa. We were brought to familiarity with the scriptures through family devotions at the dinner table and various bible lessons. Sometime around the age of fifteen, I was in my bedroom alone, and I picked up a bible. While I was browsing its contents, God's presence came through the pages and filled me with a holy awe. This made such an impression upon me, that I remembered the event years later.

About a year later, I was eager to daily digest one of those large bible storybooks from cover to cover. I felt from somewhere inside that I wanted to have a bible of my own, and so upon a visit to a city bookstore, I bought one. It had a crimson cover, and the words of Jesus were in red. Every evening after chores were done, I would read the gospels.

After I had finished with college life, I sought for a job in the city of Rotorua. I obtained a job in a mechanical workshop and moved into the city in June of 1986, boarding in Malfroy Road. Even here away from home for the first time, I had an inner desire to seek God, and so I attended the Presbyterian Church up on the hill.

After a few months, I moved into another boarding situation on Ford Road. Here, the lady was nice for the first two days, but then after that turned into a 'dragon lady'. From this affliction, I obtained a new abode in Bellingham Crescent. I moved in on Tuesday, and on Saturday at about one o'clock, there came a knock at the door. I had been reading my bible in my bedroom. I answered the door and two men stood there who were on visitation from the local Bible Baptist Church. The lady of the house, after learning their business, turned away, but I was strangely drawn toward them and sat down on the doorstep to hear what they had to say.

Pastor O. and Peter went over the bible plan of salvation with me and I prayed right there, asking the Lord Jesus Christ to save my soul. After I had prayed, Pastor O. asked me if I would look Peter in the eye and confess what I had done, confirming the deed. I did and confessed Christ as my new Savior. They then asked me if I wanted to go with them and play some tennis – I said no. After their departure, the lady made a frivolous remark about them, but I went back into my room and began to re-read the bible book of First John. And so, this is the account of my salvation experience on the fifteenth of November nineteen-eighty-six.

Here is a good lesson for us: I was raised a well-mannered teen, going to church, yet being outside the union; talking kind and yet also cursing; praying religiously and yet not knowing Him. I knew there was something missing inside, yet I could not pinpoint the what. How many people are in the same dire way?

I went to the Bible Baptist Church the next day and walked into a sweet family atmosphere. Here was good solid instruction from the bible with a dynamic song service. Here was preaching that met the need of the soul and for the first time I began to understand the meaning of many scripture passages. The folk were all sweet, inviting me to lunches and dinners for fellowship. In fact, this bonding in the homes kept this single guy in the church.

A few weeks later, I moved to a flat in Carnot Street. This was a special time for this new babe in Christ. it was here that I grew in intimately with the Lord Himself. It was while living here that two Jehovah Witnesses visited me one morning. I opened the door, my face beaming – they were startled and one asked, are you a Born-Again Christian? I confessed Christ to them before they left.

On the 25th of January 1987 I was baptized by full immersion in the creek near Pukehangi Road, Rotorua City. Pastor K. performed the ceremony. Between this time and the end of 1989, I moved a few more times. I flatted with two young men in Eruera Street for eighteen months, and although the period was not without some buffeting, I grew in the faith with their aid. I then flatted with another brother for about a year, before moving into a house in Sunset Road. Here for me, the sun did set as I settled down with good brothers in the Lord.

It was during these years that my Christian brothers and I participated in children's ministries in the church. We would fill up our vehicles with kids from the neighbouring suburbs and transport them to club activities during the week. The church was marching! Many of these kids prayed the sinner's prayer and attended Sunday School.

The children that I was assigned to pick up each week in my Ford Cortina, grew attached to me. There were so many of them who were special, but there was an inner circle of kids like Cheree, Cheryl, Tepora, and Pania.

During these years, Pastor O. and the brethren aided me in executing gospel pamphlet drops in my home region: Galatea and Murupara. Murupara is a small town about an hour's drive south of Rotorua City. We also held some campaigns in the town of Murupara with gospel singing, door-knocking, and church services. We saw a few people saved during these efforts, including my eldest brother.

February 1990

Pastor O. resigned as pastor of the church tonight, amid a church split. He had wanted to address the baptism issue of certain members, but they would have nothing to do with it. Oh, how injurious this matter has been to me. Pastor O. is like a father to me.

The Lord has been stirring my heart lately, unsettling me over my lapse condition. I desire to obey Him, but I have kept my hand on the steering wheel. I have read about the English preacher, Charles Spurgeon, and his story has encouraged me to consecrate my life to the Lord. I have made this commitment today. I ask that the Lord take my life and use it as He wills. This is the month of my consecration.

April 1990

Weeks have passed now since the church split and I am slowly being healed by the Lord. My Lord is so good to me: he is my high tower, seeing far down the road. He maneuvers my life for His pleasure. I give myself into His capable hands. It is good for me to remember that my life here is brief and that I should do the best that I can with what I have. All trials are but for a moment. Soon I shall be with the King.

I had the opportunity to bring my first public sermon in the mid-week meeting with clear utterance. I asked for nervousness to flee and so it did. The brethren were encouraged through all this. I brought a message on John 20:24-31.

God has refreshed my desire for the people in my hometown of Murupara. This fifth outreach gospel tract drop has yielded visible results with the salvation of souls. The Lord has laid it upon my heart to preach down in this mission field. It is exciting to feel the movement of the Lord. He holds my hand and shall not fail. I am accepted and loved. How dare I hold this salvation within myself, but rather with God's strength I will let it come forth, flowing words of truth and love, justice and mercy. Oh, let hearts sing of His wondrous ways, hearts that would otherwise mourn in misery; lost and without hope. Oh, how I would that God would use me to turn people to Him, who turns and changes lives and destinies.

May 1990

Following are extracts from a letter to my eldest brother who had been saved during Easter weekend.

I am writing this letter to help you to go on for Jesus. I have seen people fall away back into the world and I do not want you to succumb to that. We need to learn to rely upon God to help us to go forward. I urge you to read the bible and pray every day. This will aid you immensely to walk in the light with God.

I will tell you a little about what has happened to me. While living on the farm in Galatea, I was being drawn to seek God. I bought a bible and read it to learn more about God. In Rotorua, I went to the Presbyterian Church but was not filled there. Going into a church building does not mean that one is in right standing with God. On the 15th of November 1986, two men knocked on my door and told me how to be saved by the blood of the Lamb. I realized what I needed to do and prayed there and then. God enveloped me and assured me that I had become His own. God has been a constant friend since then, teaching and working in my life for good.

I pray for you to follow the Father, for if you remain faithful, your rewards are great. When we are in Heaven for five years, fifty years, or more, then the things of this temporal life will seem unimportant. How sad then if we have wasted our opportunity to follow Christ. Yours in Christ's love.

June 1990

I have given a brief letter to my spiritual father, Pastor O. before he returns to the United States. It reads: this letter is to say thank you for the support, instruction, and fellowship. May the Lord use you greatly as he did on the 15th of November 1986. My prayers go with you. You mean a great deal to me. Yours in Christ's love.

July 1990

The Lord has given into my care a certain group of children who have blessed me so much. After church, we usually go to the Rotorua Lakefront, or to McDonalds, or to Kurau Park. Then we usually go back to my house on Sunset Road and relax for the rest of the afternoon.

August 1990

I looked on my right hand and beheld, but there was no man that would know me: refuge failed me; no man cared for my soul. Psalm 142:4

Let no one say that no one cares for my soul – let that be our motto. Oh, what sad words to be uttered by a sinner who could have been witnessed to in the day of opportunity; or by a brother in the Lord, left lonely and failing. Let us therefore be diligent in giving our service. Oh, what a life could be lived if we would yield to the Father's sovereignty: what excitement, what sowing in tears, what wisdom, and what peace would be our experience in Him. We are brought low, but not trodden down, distraught within, but not forgotten, feeling alone, but not forsaken. The path that He has for us is as sure as He is.

This life upon this earth is but a vapor: a brief and final time of sojourn. Therefore, I have concluded that we need to live this life to its fullest potential. Alas, so many walk through life defeated, bound by vices, ignorant and somber. It's not meant to be like that, for as children of the living God, we can have all that He desires to bestow.

I have also concluded that as a child of God, the quality of this life is not determined by external circumstances but by my will; by how I choose to act and react. We need to observe past obstacles and view the goal. If we can lift our eyes, then we will see that nothing hinders us from the abundant life except our own will, which is probably soaking in unbelief. Let us lift it from the mire, and faith standing upon God's Word will wring it dry.

I have read about the lives of the bible characters. Yes, they sometimes failed, but their wills remained open to the Lord and His program. I have noted the lives of others in history and the same is true of them. This then is the key to the abundant life: to choose to persevere until the end. If we shut our will to the Lord, then we hinder the working of His special plan in our lives. The heart-cry of every Christian should be for holiness: to be like Christ. Let this then be our desire, to say that we need Him like we need oxygen to breathe like the flower needs the sun: we need Him or else we die!

As people of God, let us receive each day as a gift from above. Let us redeem the time and use it wisely. Let us hear God speak through His Word saying, come see my promises; come learn my promises; come stand upon my promises, and then you shall see what great things the Lord can do.

November 1990

Today, being a Saturday, realizing the lukewarmness of my heart was affecting my life, I resigned myself to set this day apart to spend with God in prayer and fasting. I woke up early and spent the day in my room. I read the American preacher, David Brainerd's journal, and received immense inspiration from it. At night I spent more valuable time in earnest prayer. Tears welled up in my eyes as I was moved for the broken people around me: the poor souls in Rotorua and in my homeland.

December 1990

I travelled to the town of Murupara (the area I have code-named M.A.G.A. – Murupara and Galatea area) and cycled around the streets. I noticed young people, bored and roaming without hope. My Father has burdened me for this place. I know and accept His call to be used of Him here.

In the afternoon, I went to visit my brother on the family farm. It was a hot day, so I went to the back of the farm to pray, and 'practice preach' to the river which uttered back with the sound of churning waters. God blessed my soul, and I was able to take a reflection on my life. It is good to sit and think about where one is in life and where one hopes to go in the future.

June 1991

On the 7th, I left the Bible Baptist Church and joined the Independent Baptist Church, located in the center of town. I have prayed a lot for this decision, and I have peace and liberty to do it. I have nothing against anyone in the original branch and I love them all. God has opened the door to come to this new church branch and help them in the work.

This Sunday I arose early and prayed in secret until mid-morning. God gave me special comfort. The church service in the new church branch was lively with the Spirit moving in our midst. Pastor W. gave a powerful message that stirred us in our hearts. For the first time in a while, I was moved to tears during the sermon invitation. A man went up to the front and I was able to take him outside and lead him to the Lord. Glory to God!

August 1991

My dad went in for his scheduled heart by-pass operation. The surgeon encountered difficulty and about mid-afternoon, my dad's-tired body yielded to death. I was notified and traveled to meet with family, the Lord being a special comfort and shield to me in my time of need.

The departure of a loved one is hard to bear, but we find comfort in friends and consolation in our God. Dad was a man who encouraged a work ethic and a moral compass in his children. He was a farmer, carpenter, and engineer: in all practical works, he prospered. I got to know him best in the last two years. I had asked him about his relationship with God, and he gave an answer of his assurance.

Here we see the frailty of life and the certainty of death. Life is too short to live thoughtlessly. Whereas you know not what shall be on the morrow. For what is your life? It is even a vapor that appears for a little time and then vanishes away. James 4:14

September 1991

I heard about the Lord supplying a building for the church people to meet in. There are living quarters for Ashley and me, rooms, and an auditorium for the church services. The building is in a central location and is at a decent price.

I am teaching Sunday school for the 8–12-year-olds. God has burdened me afresh for the real needs: souls and God's pleasure. No material thing binds me tonight. I have been reading the biography of the famous missionary, Hudson Taylor, and I am inspired by his ministry. Patience is a hard lesson to learn. How hard too for Jesus the carpenter, having to wait for the due time to go and preach. I must wait for the appointed time too.

I have been rising early for prayer and it is making a significant difference to my day. I was brought to sorrowful tears at the laziness and lack of concern over souls. I committed myself into God's hands, asking Him to subdue corruption within me. I need to get to business, the Lord's business. Work needs to be done and a mission accomplished. I shall not rest until it is done, and my own eyes have seen it come about. My heart is filled with joy and pleasure in my God.

In the church youth club, I was able to lead a boy to the Lord with prayer. Many children come and their hearts are open to the things of God.

I have been rising at six every morning to be with my sweet Lord. The benefits are manifest: my walk is closer; my peace is secure, and my joy fixes itself in Him. God says I love them that love me, and those that seek me early shall find me. When I fail to meet with God, I feel empty, but when I do, I am satisfied and equipped for the challenges of the day.

A wonderful day in church with a powerful message. The presence of God was strong. A man accepted Christ during the sermon invitation and many of us knelt at the altar. I committed myself at the altar and then arose and made a profession of my decision to serve the Lord full-time. The pastor spoke to the congregation and insisted upon their prayers for my training in the ministry.

October 1991

What peace, what perfect rest we can have in Jesus. He made me realize this morning regarding the selling of the car, that it is His car and therefore His responsibility to sell it (as I work with Him). Perfect peace flooded my soul as this dawned upon me. Likewise, it is the same with His mission through me: it is His responsibility to open and close doors, to guide and supply, to correct and to convert. But seek ye first the kingdom of God, and his righteousness; and all these things shall be added unto you. Faith in action is the key to the fulfillment of promises and blessings. Unbelief robs us, but faith opens the door to soul rest.

God's gift to me has been abiding peace: peace that has not left me since I gave my all into His hands a few days ago. Tonight, as I lay in bed, I was in the Spirit. The Lord showed me what it really was to be one with Him: it was so wonderful. I pray that I will never lose His presence.

God enabled me to pour out my heart in prayer for holiness and commitment in myself, and for God's people in this town, that we would experience revival. Oh, that hearts would be softened toward God and carnality subdued: that missions be opened. God has burdened my heart for this great need of the Church. I will pray continually until God sends His anointing for service. Doors will open shortly, and the Lord is going to do a great work.

Absolute blessed Sunday, with good unity among the brethren and with the best time of singing I have experienced in a long time. Enthusiastic preaching with good times of fellowship.

November 1991

Today is my fifth birthday in the Lord. I have taken the day off work and am on my way to M.A.G.A. As I write, I am in a secluded spot near the main highway. This day is for the Lord and me to spend together. Here is my devotion to Jesus.

Five years have passed since you came into my life. I shudder to think of what life would be like without you. How pleasant it is to know you; what a privilege it is to belong to you. I remember the days of preparation: eighteen years on the Galatea farm. I then moved to Rotorua on June 9th, 1986, and a few months later in Bellingham Crescent, you stepped into my life.

My heart was soft; your word took root. The devil was not able to snatch, the sun was not able to scorch, and the thorns were not able to stifle. By faith in your beloved Son, the light pierced through unto justification. No more night, no more searching, and no more thirsting: I am satisfied. And I have experienced prayers answered, powerful preaching, and delicious teaching of the word. I have traced your hand upon my life and felt your touch upon my heart. I know your desire to use me in M.A.G.A. – this is my mission. I am no longer content to just sit and waste my life: my days flee as a shadow.

December 1991

The Lord has opened a door for me to work a part-time job with a Christian brother so that I can go through years of Bible Institute training. This brother has forgotten my wages for this week and so I am doing a little exercise (like the missionary Hudson Taylor did) to just pray that God would jog his memory. This will work to strengthen my faith in my God.

Chapter Two: The Awakening Years

This chapter covers the period of the Pilgrim Preachers second set of five years in the BBC Movement. The sapling is sprouting in the orchard of a good local church. Here, we begin to receive formal training to prepare for the future mission. Come with me on this journey...

January 1992

I weep when I see my failure before my God. I seem so reluctant to just completely cast myself into His hands. He calls and I do not listen; He wants to use me, and I turn away. But the majesty on high still loves me and desires to work on me to make me more like Christ. There is hope for me I feel, for the Lord assures me, and my vision is to be greatly used by Him, whom I now fail.

We had our debut church service in the new church building (on View Road) with an excellent spirit among us. I am also preparing to start the Pilgrim's Progress Club in a few weeks for the children.

March 1992

I was very sick last Sunday and was not able to begin the Pilgrim's Progress Club for the children. The Lord kept me in bed and counseled me concerning my walk with Him. This is His club, and I must be one with Him. This Sunday, we began the club, and two kids made a commitment to Christ. Bible Institute also began this week with a number of classes commencing on primary topics.

April 1992

The church held a sunrise service on Easter Sunday morning. In the afternoon, four people were baptized. During the evening church service, I preached my first sermon in the new building, taking as my text Ephesians chapter two.

May 1992

BBC pastors came from all over the nation, converging on our new building for the Pastor's Fellowship Conference this weekend. We enjoyed good preaching, fellowship, and buffet meals (lamb on a spit). I gave my testimony during one service. The pastors agreed to pray for revival and to have better communication between themselves.

July 1992

O Lord, lately I have not been faithful to you. I have not bowed the knee before you. The pastor preached a message that rebuked me. I laughed, but now I have sobered up. It has all come from allowing secular music back into my life. It has become my golden calf which I have danced around. Sin and backsliding came in gradually, but the Lord has come in like a flaming arrow, piercing me to tears of godly sorrow.

God is great and ready to pardon me. He is precious to me once more. In one day, I have been turned around to walk in the path of peace. I wash me in the fountain. Jesus appears before me. He takes my hand. I feel His warmth of compassion flow down my arm and touch the rest of me. His smile breaks my heart of stone. I feel clean.

August 1992

It is not up to us to lead and scheme, plan, and strive, but simply follow. Who knows of tomorrow? He knows. Do you know your future down to the last detail? He knows. Can you tell your lifespan down to the last minute? He knows.

He is best to lead. Who are you to usurp yourself? He is all-knowing, all-powerful, and all-seeing. When He speaks, the earth trembles, the mountains shake, and the sea rolls back its tide. There is nothing hidden from His eyes; nowhere to escape His view of you; no rock to hide beneath. There is no hindrance to His mighty arm: what He wills, He does.

He has the capabilities to lead; you do not have the needed prerequisites. All you can do is to throw up your feeble, mortal hands in helplessness and acknowledge Him, saying, guide me O gentle Savior; teach me, O precious Lord!

September 1992

Oh to be a Father-pleaser. That in the early morning as we wake, we might say, today, I will be a Father-pleaser. For that is what He wants us to say: that we desire to please Him. He wants us to let Him live His life in and through us; to let Him guide our feet to where He would have us go and to teach our lips to speak right things. So that at night when we pillow our heads, we can say, today, I have allowed Jesus His right to live in and through me: yea I have been a Father-pleaser.

October 1992

I have been asleep in liberty like the Israelites in the days of the judges: going around in a circle of sin, oppression, repentance, liberty, and sin. I have been in bondage: oppression took hold of me. I feared it would never let me go. I cried out to God for deliverance, let me loose and I shall serve thee. He did in power and rejoiced my heart in praise.

But in the process of time, I left my first love again: my heart sagged in the faith; my mind was turned away by various persuasions of the deceiver's corps. I slept in liberty when I should have been at work; I wasted precious time when I should have been redeeming it, and I failed the Lord when I should have been pleasing Him. I lost honour and respect during my sleeping hours. I got used to the darkness. This is not my home: I am a child of the Light! Arise, therefore! I will go forth to do my Lord's will.

This last year has been one of extremes: with a good start to the year with the commencement of The Pilgrim's Progress Club; with the church being in great unity, and the pastor's fellowship conference. But then through the winter, we hibernated like bears; being dormant like a volcano. Now as the sun arises to warm our days, we stir into life again.

It was back in May, that I heard about a proposed trip to visit certain churches in Indonesia and the Philippines. Now I am ready to accompany the small party who will be going. This trip overseas is God's will for me. It is like a constraining force that compels me to go. I cannot break free; neither do I desire to.

At this point in time, I believe that it is not my calling, but my lesson – for my mission is here in my native land. And I know that I shall not die, but live; I shall not perish in the distant land, but I shall return. The Lord is with me, for me, and not finished with me yet. There is much to be done in the fields. My pen refuses to lie still until I have written my last book from the shelf of my imagination.

God has given me the gift of being an author. Even in my youth, I wrote short stories and lyrics. Books had a great influence on me. I was able to identify with the characters. Today, writing is still my passion, but with a difference: the Holy Spirit inspires me and causes words to flow like a steady stream. I live and breathe, write, and work for Jesus.

I have been asked why I haven't got a girlfriend. The answer is that I have chosen to wholeheartedly follow the Lord. God has given me grace for this path, and I am content with my lot. Too often, infatuation has taken me from my first love. I cannot divide myself. God must be first, and that does not happen when a woman comes along. I have not ruled out a relationship in the future. God who is jealous for me sets up barriers and destroys my schemes to keep me on His path, to keep me as His man to accomplish the mission ahead. I know that God has a very special mission for me.

November 1992

Extracts from my letter to Pastor O. (Who had gone back to the USA).

I remember the day that you came to my door, and we sat on the step to open the Bible. I believed on Christ and took Him as my personal savior. Now years have passed, and the Lord keeps me on His path. I have seen His faithfulness; known His deeper love and walked with Him in the garden of intimacy. I have witnessed souls being saved, snatched away from hell - heard their cries of joy as they possess the life. I have seen their clothes spotted by sin, washed and made fragrant through the blood of the Lamb.

The church, I have found to be my home: there is no other place for me. The life of Christ is my life: where else could I go? God has granted me His perfect peace. I abide in sweet peace.

Thank you, my father in the faith, for coming to the shores of the 'Great White Cloud' and listening to the Spirit. I hope to see you in the flesh one day again, but if that never happens, then I know that we will embrace in that yonder fair land of Heaven. Farewell for now.

Tim has been coming along to church meetings for a while now. This Wednesday's church service has seen Tim come under conviction and a desire to seek salvation. During the sermon, the Lord showed me in a vision how he would use me to lead Tim to pray the sinner's prayer: and it came about after the service precisely to that revelation. Tim came upstairs to my flat after the service and asked me to explain in more detail the way to be born again. I showed him from the scriptures until he was ready to call upon the name of the Lord. Afterward, we went to the pastor's place to rejoice together. Tim is a pilgrim starting out, a saint of the highest God. He is but a grain of sand in the sandcastle, God has called me to build.

When I look back and see what the Lord has done for me, I marvel. God has lifted me from nothing to great abundance; taken me from wasting my life to redeeming it for His service and from loneliness to companionship. Financially, I am not well off, but I get by with the Lord, who promises to provide for His servant.

O Lord, I long for more personal holiness; I long to be near your heart. I approach you. Lift me up into your bosom and hold me close. I love you O Lord. Draw me and draw your church closer to your heart. Design us after your divine pattern. Shine your face upon us and build your church. We have such a happy group of pilgrims gathered in your name.

Thank you Lord for giving us our wonderful pastor. Keep him and direct him in the work. All we are, is because of you. We worship you. Hear the voice of our prayer and praise in your holy temple.

This December, I am off on my overseas trip to Indonesia and the Philippines to scout out a native pastor for this home church in Rotorua to support.

January 1993

Since my return from the overseas trip, a fire has been kindled in me; an earnestness; a zeal; a quickening caused by seeing the mission fields in Indonesia and the Philippines. God has fanned this fire in me, and I am no longer the same. Now there is urgency in my step; a power in my preaching; an enthusiasm never quite attained before. I have been woken up; my eyes stretched wide with a new zeal to run and not faint; go and not stay; speak and not hold back.

April 1993

God is truly living in and through me now. His presence shines from my face. I am enveloped in the Spirit's presence – it appears to me, as I look, a light shadow about my face. Men see the peaceful look on my face and praise God. Pastor W. and I are of one spirit in the work.

If this is what God has done for me thus far, then what shall the next few years bring? My eyes glisten, and my heart moves within me. There is excitement mingled with peace.

May 1993

Last weekend, the church hosted a mission conference. Portions of the video of my Indonesian trip were shown, messages were preached, and good food was partaken of. It was a good weekend with decisions made for Christ. A few of the members committed their lives more fully to Christ's service. The church members voted to financially support a native pastor in central Java.

My convert Tim has surrendered his life to full-time service. The Bible Institute has professional teaching staff with full classrooms.

August 1993

God's hand is so real upon me. He moves in my life, and I marvel. What hand is this that guides me? It is a hand of love, giving to me what I need. What hand is this that guides me? It is the hand of patience, being long-suffering toward me. What hand is this that guides me? It is the hand of strength, in which I am victorious. What hand is this that guides me? It is the hand of understanding, succoring me. For this God is my God and He is my guide through life.

Where could I have been now if God had not intervened in my life? What would I be doing now if God had not redeemed my soul? Would

I be in a good job with lots of money? But God called me away. Would I be still going to church like most bleary-eyed professors? But God called me away. I have left my nets with my dad and have gone to be a fisher of men.

I cannot rest content being a nine-to-five man: for God has called me away to be a mission-man. He has brought me along a superb path. I am not content to walk the steps of a common Christian or to live a settled life. I abhor the thought of being a pew warmer. God is calling me away. I am forever grateful to Him. He is the keeper of my heart. How can I not follow the shepherd of my life?

September 1993

I have just completed writing the six-part devotional course for new converts, called 'The Progress of the Pilgrim'. It has taken me about one year to write it down. This exercise has been beneficial for me, as it has quickly systematized my dogma on the topics covered.

Last Sunday, I preached both services while the pastor was away. I preached about the way of the pilgrim and the path set before us. God has separated me to proclaim the way of the pilgrim. He has made me a pilgrim preacher.

Rebekah has been moved to like me, and it seems the Lord is drawing us both together. God has turned my heart. I am incomplete without her companionship. She is pure and our friendship is clean. God is knitting us together. She is a writer, a poet. She knows God's faithfulness, possessing simple faith. She is a virtuous woman who prays to her Father and sees answered prayers. I asked her if she had been praying for me. She said that she had been asking if I was the one for her and the response was favorable.

The Lord must know that I need a wife: someone to love and someone to love me; someone to hold and someone to hold me. Rebekah is remarkable. Her price is far above rubies. She will do me well all the days of my life. (Rebekah is the pastor's daughter).

I have had to defend the faith lately before of various antagonists. It is my turn to hold up the banner of the Cross as did my spiritual forefathers. I am a man born one hundred years too late, for I would have loved to walk with the preachers in the great revivals. Yea, and to have helped Hudson Taylor; to have heard Charles Spurgeon preach, and to have prayed alongside David Brainerd. But God be praised. I am a man born in the time appointed. I am blessed!

October 1993

I arose at six-thirty and spent an hour in worship and meditation upon John chapter fifteen. I feel completely emptied of all vainglory and self-achievement. The Spirit's blessing is upon me again.

Lord, take my mind and teach me; Lord, take my heart and affect me; Lord, take my will and use me. Lord, most people suppress you. Lord, live in me. Let me not fall asleep in liberty. Thank you for supplying my every need. Keep me on the path – for a good Christian is a pilgrim, and a good pilgrim looks upward bound.

November 1993

This is a special month for me: the commemoration of the month when I was born again from above. This is my seventh birthday in the Lord. As I look back, I can see two great turning points in my life: one, when I left my hometown at the age of eighteen and was born again a few months later, never to be the same again. The second, was when I went on this overseas trip to Indonesia and the Philippines last December. I was woken up; my eyes stretched wide; a fire placed in my inward parts. I am not the same man as I was before the trip.

Lately, I have had the liberty to speak to those at work. One way now is if they will not come to church to hear the preaching, I will go to them and preach.

Lord, I used to be ashamed, and the devil would make me take a step back when people asked me for a reason of the hope in me. Now the awakening has occurred; the Spirit reigns in me. Those at work know where I stand, and they respect my Lord.

Some have noted that even in my pulpit preaching there has been a change. Before I was not as energetic, not as lively. But now the Spirit sets me like a violin string and plays me to the jubilant praise of the glory of His grace, or there is a thundering as the call goes out to come with me to follow Jesus, to live the life the saint was called to live.

I stood at my lofty window one night gazing at the light-lit city spread before me, my heart broken, for souls are eating and drinking, being merry, marrying and giving in marriage, not aware that the door shall suddenly close upon them soon and they shall be left outside to face divine retribution.

One night I stood alone, looking out of my lofty window at the dim-lit streets below. Many streets, many homes, and many people. In the streets, there is so much confusion, so much damage, and so much darkness. People in this town wander the streets, expressionless, cold, somber, and without hope. There are battered wives, rebellious children, and drunken fathers. There is no joy in their lives; no light is seen in their darkness. These people shall remain unclean unless one who is clean should say, Lord, here am I, send me! Yeah, who will go, who will care, who will tell?

I see broken people, ruined lives; lost and blinded people, who are separated and condemned already. I see souls searching for something permanent to fill that void inside. They are craving true love, unchanging acceptance, unfailing security, and a sure and joyful future.

Look and see as God sees. For God can see into every home and into every heart. He sees what's going on. He sees domestic abuse. He sees the street kid sniffing glue in a dark corner. He sees a group of youngsters watching a 'blue' movie. He sees the one-night stands. He sees the Christians watching television, laughing at the lust and corruption. He sees the well-paid minister eating and drinking with his friends.

But where is the prayer-warrior? Where is the soul-winner? Where is the one who does not compromise? Where is the one who exercises great faith? Yeah, who does go, who does care, who does tell? We are the servants of the living God: will you go, will you care, will you tell?

Where God is not, Satan has filled the void. And when God is rejected, Satan remains king in an individual and in a nation bowed in darkness. If an individual is seeking God, then Satan will step up his efforts and methods of blinding and binding such a person. And if the called of God procrastinate, Satan will get in first: his ministers will come in smart attire, faces bright, eloquent speech, deceiving the ignorant. They are militant, knocking on doors.

December 1993

Rebekah wrote me a note affirming her love for me. She accepts me and I feel secure in her love. We are in a relationship now and look forward to a future together. She is of a high spiritual caliber; a good gift from Heaven.

The Lord has been speaking to me lately about prayer. I asked Him to teach me to pray and to give me the great blessing: a fresh anointing for service. I have been in the woods on the farm, in the presence of God. As a result, many prayer requests have been answered. I am experiencing freedom in the spiritual walk. Liberty comes by absolute trust and obedience to the Lord's directives. This is contrary to human logic, but the person entering in will find it so. God has enlarged the space around me and blessed me in so many ways. He has anointed my prayer life. He has taught me to be a servant. My goal is His glory: the working out of His divine plan.

This has been a good year. God has kept me safe and healthy, and though not wealthy; I have enough. Pastor W. and I are good friends, and the church family is closely knit. Through institute classes, I have increased in knowledge and have had my eyes opened to see a bigger perspective on Christendom. Pastor W. has helped me to grow, in that he has stood back and allowed me to take on responsibilities in the church roles.

January 1994

A most fabulous day in quite a while. Both church services were filled with soul-stirring power and good responses. Folks went forward to the altar to make re-dedications. I have been praying for the anointing, both for myself and the pastor. We need a revival in the church. I need a fresh anointing. I am clean and ready and desirous. I cannot go on merely existing without it. I don't want to lose it again: it is too painful.

I am in the habit of going into the House of God and falling prostrate down beside the pulpit to pour out my heart to God. Many times, I have been carried along by the Spirit in trembling intercession. I still need more love to be a servant, more power to be a soul-winner, and more of Jesus in my life to be an example to my children. Oh, that I could just obtain a little of what those saints in the golden age of missions had. They were the jewels in the crown of the church age. Therefore God, give me your plan in my life, or give me death!

February 1994

I had trouble today, as work did not go well. And except I was with the Spirit, I would have succumbed to depression. Demonic activity set against me to detract me from the victory won last night. The prayer series that I am teaching in the church is working effectually upon many member's hearts. God was honored, Satan bruised, and I hid behind the Cross.

I thank my God because I am still in plan A. God's first desire is being worked out in my life. I know many who have forfeited God's best for something less. May God continue to preserve me on the pilgrim pathway. Now I find myself in a good thing: looking forward on the path with a clearer vision. I am focused on the 'cross-country race' set before me. I have only one ambition and I am seeing it played out day by day. I see myself in the years to come being in a traveling circuit-preaching ministry. My heart is for my countrymen.

May 1994

I have been teaching my original work, 'The Pilgrim's Prayer-life' series, during the mid-week church services. We are experiencing the closest thing to revival in the church that I know. People are getting their hearts right with God and each other. Many go forward during the sermon invitations to kneel at the altar. Folks are determined to serve the Lord and witness the gospel. Three-quarters of the members have committed themselves to some form of ministry. Fellowship is truly sweet in the church. A number of souls have been saved. People are revived – praise God!

Rebekah gave me a note in Bible Institute this morning, saying that she loves me more now as we have grown to know each other better. I sent her some roses. Rebekah helps me in teaching our Sunday School class, as well as accompanying me on church visits. She just drops everything to go with me to do the work of the ministry.

June 1994

Revival is in the church. The people are full of love and concern for each other. We are one, striving together for the faith of the gospel. Unsaved folks are coming in during our Sunday services and being moved by the sermons.

July 1994

Pastor W. is away in Indonesia, and I am helping to look after the church during his absence. I used to be a man of war, struggling with various sins, but now God has expanded my borders like Solomon's kingdom, giving me peace all around.

Over this month, I have been preaching about revival. There has been an effect as one asked to be baptized, and others have come forward to the pulpit altar weeping.

August 1994

Pastor W. has returned from Indonesia, and he is awakened. He has seen the teeming millions in that land yet untold. Our church supports missionaries in Java. Pastor W. is keen to start a mission work in Tokoroa, a large town West of Rotorua city. We are both praying for that with the aim that I will eventually take it over and run with it.

My sweet Rebekah has passed away in her sleep, during a seizure. We are all devastated by this sudden event. My soulmate has left, and I am all alone. I am laid prostrate on the floor and feel the worst kind of pain in my gut. My eyes are a river of tears; a fountain that breaks forth at random. Already I miss her laugh, her manner, her words, and her presence.

Rebekah, you were the sunshine of our lives; that sparkle of joy. You live on in our memories; your life has touched ours. Goodbye for now, until we meet again yonder. I love you; I miss you.

September 1994

Oh Father, this nation has rejected you and cast you aside for vanity and gods which cannot save. But there is a remnant that looks to you; there are people who care. Preserve us in your ways; bind us together. Help us to endure unto the end. Father, use this generation of believers. Give us understanding in your scriptures, an intimate devotional life, and a steadfast heart upon our special missions.

Two were saved at the kids club this week. Four people want to be baptized this coming Sunday. The church is growing in every way. Pastor W. preaches with the anointing upon him, hitting the nails on the head so tactfully. God is moving in His house, searching the hearts: repentance and confessions abound.

I went for a drive around the towns of Putaruru and Tokoroa, and I am excited at how a circuit could be maintained for a preacher. My heart is moved for my nation like never before. A vision for the greater region is before my eyes now.

We have more full-time students in Bible Institute. Work is proceeding on the church building with various renovations being undertaken.

Since Rebekah's departure, I have been an empty shell, walking and performing my duties but with a hole inside. I have been brought down and humbled completely: there is nothing left in me. God has used His scriptures to meet my heart-cries and comfort me. He is sovereign and is working out a plan that will be seen clearer in years to come. He is working out the servant-hood lesson in my life at present. Heaven seems so much more inviting now: that land is so much sweeter. I can't wait to go there to behold it all, to thank my King, and to embrace

Rebekah again. Although I weep, I can't do much about it. All the crying in the world will not bring her back. So, I must endure until the end. Rebekah, meet me at the gates.

October 1994

Satan has had an advantage over me for I have felt neglected by Pastor W. I met with the pastor and told him how I feel. He is still greatly affected over the loss of his daughter, Rebekah. With this communication, the weight has been lifted; all is sweet peace now. Oh, what a relief to have it all released. Oh, to think that I have grieved the pure Spirit and hindered His working in the church. Please, O God, continue the revival in the church.

Through this experience, I have realized that I am not ready to go out into my mission. I am not sure that I am called to be a pastor either. I know that I am called to preach, yet I don't possess the gifts or mindset of a regular pastor. This needs to be settled before I embark: a shaky foundation will cause me to lean over. God is interested in me, and I love Him because He is working on me to make me better.

With the sudden influx of new people into the church, unity has suffered. By dealing with their transition from the old life to the new walk and accepting each other, warts and all – these disturbances have taken their toll. The revival spirit has almost disappeared. We must recommit ourselves to seek it afresh.

November 1994

The devil is causing much strife in the church. There is a Māori family who are a bunch of thieves, and two families are feuding. God has given me a new friend at this time, who has become an oasis in the desert. My mind has been perplexed these last few months since my soul-mates departure. The toughest period is the months after the decease when it all hits home. The grieving process renders the mind ineffective for focus.

December 1994

Jesus died for me. What shall I give Him in return? Oh, to reach out to lost souls for whom He died and to win for the Lamb that was slain the reward of His suffering! I was helpless and hopeless when He came to deliver me. He was a servant with a missionary heart of love. My heart now burns within me; my tears are my food as I consider the state of Christendom. Oh, what shall I do? The land is in such a dire state, and I am only one man.

June 1995

In the last few weeks since God has revealed His specific will concerning MAGA (Murupara and Galatea Area), my focus has turned to that mission. I have been afflicted by demonic powers. I have been troubled regarding the restraint of my views, liberty, and expression. I want to be in MAGA and that is where I am living presently (in thought), but I am no earthly good here while in that frame of mind. I fight men and ultimately fight God; I blame men and ultimately blame God. I need rather to give my best while here, and also prepare for that awesome future task.

The fields are white and wasting. Souls are perishing in the fields while we rest in the house. Let us rise to the work, for the Master is coming. How will He weep when He sees His harvest is not reaped? How will He respond when He sees that His trusted workers were careless and idle? Oh Jesus, my master, let me be active in the field. In the harvest now ripened there is a place for me. I hear His voice calling. I cannot help but respond. I love the Christ who in His body bore all of my shame. He set me free to love souls wandering like lost sheep over the mountains bare.

Lord, share your burden with me. Let me carry the cross with you. I desire to go the whole way as you did. Let me accomplish my mission. Teach me to be a soul-winner. This is my prayer. I want to be consistent in bearing fruit. I am tired of being barren. Work your plan in and through me for your good pleasure. Oh, joy of my heart, apple of my eye, reason for my existence – let me bring to you rewards for your suffering, payments for your time of passion. Let me burn out for Jesus!

July 1995

The annual Baptist Winter Camp was a time of refreshing, concreting relationships and convictions. My brother was moved to consecrate his life to the Lord for some form of future service.

The Lord has been calling me to deeper worship, with blessed experiences in the prayer closet. On Sunday, Pastor W. preached from the text John 4:24, and I was pleased that God had confirmed His word unto His servant.

I went into the supermarket and my Lord opened the door for me to get a job there. His timing is perfect, and I am jubilant in praise. He is in control, and I abide under the shadow of His wing.

August 1995

(Extracts from a letter sent out to various peers around the country).

I hope that you are still progressing in the true faith; battling the resilient enemy. Remember that perishing souls depend upon you to bring them the message of deliverance. I meditate upon bible characters and glean encouragement from their example to stand firm in the way. Let us join together in prayer for this nation steeped in the darkest gloom: for as we gaze to the west, judgment looms from the east. Let us respond to the call of the Lamb to service before He smites as the Lion.

May you be blessed always in the center of His will. We are the church of tomorrow.

God saw my doubting, confusion, and distress of mind, so He lovingly gave me a more perfect view of my mission. He talked with me about raising a band of pilgrim evangelists, who will go out in the fashion of the historic Lollards and the Moravians to evangelize this nation.

How will I enter MAGA? I will take time off work and go into MAGA to intercede, conduct analysis, make initial contacts, and see if a door opens for a job. If a job comes up, then I will move into the town as directed by the Lord. If no job surfaces during the period, then I will condense my working days and begin a cell group in the town.

The Lord was pleased to meet with me tonight in a special way. Oh, to abide in His presence and never leave. Oh, to be losing more and more control and let Him take up the slack. Oh Lord, draw me more into yourself so that I may know you better. Lay your hand upon me and use me again. I fail your trust so often and fail your love so commonly. Oh, make me faithful so that you can deposit your precious gifts to me. Make me responsible so that I might be filled with your greatest treasure. Search me, heal me, and establish me in faithfulness evermore.

September 1995

I had a mighty season in prayer tonight. The Lord was most gracious to let me be restored back into His presence after being held in 'doubting castle' for the last few weeks. The devil had me in his snare and I had forgotten about the key to God's promise. I was able to pour out my heart affectionately for the unsaved. An awesome presence accompanied my pleadings and I found favour in God's sight. I felt love go through me like waves. Oh, how pleasant it is to dwell in the secret place; in His pavilion of strength.

My heart is snared by a certain woman. I am exceedingly grieved because I want her, but the Lord won't suffer me to have her. I am blue and cast down. I told her that I like her, and she has replied to me favorably. I can have her if I want. But the Lord speaks to me and cuts me off, and I mourn. I am so lonely, and I wish to learn of her.

I have suffered the loss of many things in my pilgrimage in order to win Christ and to know Him more intimately. I have MAGA before my eyes and I know the devil fears the success of the mission and the power that could be displayed through me. God is my high tower. He knows best. He says no, and my heart burns like the green hills on fire.

October 1995

We have had marvelous Sunday services lately as the sun rises to warm our days and hearts. Anna, my faithful student in class, has been a more productive soul-winner than I, with many friends coming along with her to church. The new Bible Institute principal has arrived and is settling into his role. Pastor W. is comforted and revived in his work.

I reflect and cannot count all of the blessings which I enjoy at present. I am full. The Lord has inspired me to sow seed at every opportunity at my workplace.

God keeps calling me back when I stray. He draws me in various ways when I neglect Him. He won't let me go. In reflection I see Him moving to impart goodness. Precious souls are not hanging on me, but rather on the power, wisdom, and love that is channeled through me. If I falter as a vessel in the devotional life, then the flow of the divine gift is crimped: morbidity and rashness result. I wish to be a faithful servant of God.

God is so good to me. I have known Him for nine years and He has been everything that He said and more to me. I am glad that this God is my God. Amen and amen!

Pastor W. preached hard this morning on soul-winning and the apathy of Christians. Afterward, I contacted Andrew, a workmate, and invited him to the evening church service. After the service, we had supper together and he decided to take Christ as his savior.

I determined in my heart to ask out the woman. Many times, I endeavored to ask her out, but I had no divine enablement. I am brought to realize that truly, without Him, I can do nothing, and against Him, I find it arduous. I am bought with a price to glorify Him. I have vowed myself to Him on numerous occasions and He holds me to my vow.

Truly, if I pass through this temptation, there will be nothing for me to boast in. Only by grace will I continue on my pilgrim pathway to accomplish the mission. Great is the faithfulness of the majestic God. I will love Him because He first loved me.

My workmate, Andrew, though saved, has not made it back to church yet. Simon, another workmate, came to see me two nights ago because he had been shaken up by a near-fatal accident. He asked many questions and decided to put Christ off for a more convenient day. Troy, another workmate, came to visit me tonight and after many questions, decided to receive Jesus as redeemer. We also had three children saved in the youth club this week.

November 1995

I have been in a conflict lately. There is the great weight of the future mission and its apparent difficulties. There is the thought of separating from these church people. The most important thing for me is to remain in the choicest plan of God for me. MAGA is where God wants me to be. If I run, I will lose the best. Oh Lord, give me a faith like Abrahams. There is a door to open to MAGA. Only a faith like

Abrahams can use the opportunity. I have failed many times. I don't want to fail big time.

MAGA seems such folly. What earthly good can come out of MAGA? What is there in that town? What a waste! What can come out of MAGA? A pilgrim band!

Oh God, add thousands of kiwis to the bride of Christ before you return. Sweep across this land in one last mighty revival. As the pilgrim band sweeps over this land, may the cry be, 'No retreat; no surrender!' No retreat from the face of our enemies; no surrender of our beliefs, values and standards.

Every mission must have obstacles and close calls. Every good story sees the good guy facing obstacles before the victory comes. So, it is in life. To appreciate the Lord's power and grace, we too must endure hardships, temptations and testings before we reach the finish line and receive the reward.

Oh I wish I had a deeper love. Paul wished himself accursed for his countrymen. I wish I could go through harm and hurt in order that my countrymen would be delivered. Oh, to die to self more, to pay the price, to endure hardness, to ford the river, to go where I am called. Oh, I wish I had a deeper love.

Oh how I have learnt that I am a man marked by God. He preserves me and walks with me. He desires to powerfully convert the heathen through my weakness. I am marked for the appointment, and I know that is why I live. If I fall out of plan A, life will be most miserable. I shiver at the thought. God has revealed to me the pilgrim philosophy that I would impart it to others. May God be blessed as His plan unfolds.

I went to visit Marcus, a workmate, and sat with him expounding the scriptures until he joyfully took Christ as his savior. I want this man for the pilgrim band as he is a pilgrim already and keen on street out reach He is leaving shortly to join the armed forces even though I would prefer him to enlist in the Kings' army.

I have been having daily fellowship with Marcus and Andrew. They both came to the service on Wednesday night, and I preached 'When Euroclydon comes'. The spirit moved and stilled many hearts in soul searching.

I spent this day in prayer, fasting, and writing. The Lord ministered to me in a special way and counseled me concerning His strength for my calling, much like He did for Joshua. His presence and peace were in my dwelling, and we talked about the future.

In the autumn of 1986, I was in a tight spot. I needed a job, and a door opened with work and board in the city of Rotorua. In 1991 I desired to go through Bible College and God opened a door for me to work part-time with enough provision to get me through the four years of training. Is it going to be any different in the future? Has my God changed? And just to make the assurance doubly sure, God has delivered me again by providing a job in the supermarket, one year before I take up my appointment.

I have urged the Bible Institute principal to push me through to graduation before the winter of 1996, but he has reasoned against me and the plan.

December 1995

I see the clouds of darkness above, driven by the winds of the fierceness of God's wrath. Hovering over, holding the judgement. Oh, the divine patience! Lord, I can't stop these clouds. I can't hold back the coming rain. God, revive me again. Lord, I can't run ahead of them alone, but in the Spirit, hope is present. I want to run for you. I want to run ahead of the clouds to shout and to warn the sinners to turn.

Lord as I cry out for you to raise up a pilgrim band, you shined the light in the very spot on the horizon. Yea Lord, let me live leaning on your breast and die in your arms. Let me never say no to the One who said yes to the tree and all it entailed.

Once again we come to Christmas time where we give things to people. Things do not make people permanently happy. What makes a person happy is the love of the giver. And there is one who has both loved and given, and yet we esteem Him not. This Christmas I celebrate your coming, oh Lord. I am grateful that you came and entered into your mission. If you had not, then I would be lost in the blackest night. Let me be faithful also.

March 1996

There is another lady whom I desire to date, but the Lord who changes not, still does not want me to attach myself to anything this side of MAGA. The lady knows that I like her, but it has not been taken further. She waits for me, but I am constrained by my master. Last time, God had to put the restraints on full power to stop me, but this time I remember the agony and submit myself to my first love. I want to be a good pilgrim and fulfill my mission. The Lord, like a parent with a teenager, is giving me more freedom this time to exercise free will.

April 1996

After reading the missionary Adoniram Judson's biography, the Lord said to me that there are two principles that make missions work: a fire and a thirst. And that is the problem in this country: neither is in large abundance. There is a lack of fire in the bosom of the saint and a thirst in the being of the sinner. Both compel action. But if there is no present action, then in the time of the end, the sinner shall thirst in the everlasting fire, and the saint's work shall be tried by fire, and then both thirst for a second chance.

Because Jesus lives, I live, and I shall never see the smoke of fire arise continually; never feel with excruciation the flames lick their sting into every nook of my being. I shall never hear the shrieks of like wretched beasts wishing to find the inside handle to the door of physical death.

Chapter Three: The Maga Years

This chapter covers the period of the Pilgrim Preachers divine internship. The trunk is strengthened as the man is taken into isolation with God.

M.A.G.A. = Murupara and Galatea Area.

May 1996

I travelled to Murupara to consider the condition of the town. It has certainly fallen from its former glory, now with high unemployment. Hope has dimmed for the young, with drugs and crime rampant. The conditions are ripe to recruit pilgrim workers. I drove around the town to view the place. I am like a missionary entering a native country. I take this mission seriously: people need the Lord!

I took time off work and went to stay in MAGA for this week. I spent time in praise, self-examination, and intercession. The Spirit of peace came down in blessing and everything I do here is worked together for good. With immense inspiration, I wrote the 'Know to Glow' publication.

On Thursday I went into the town centre and put my name down for a job in the superette. The next day I heard that I was to have an interview. I accepted the job offer and the shock of change came over me. I begged God for courage, wisdom, and assurance at this time, for He must go with me as surely as He has gone before me.

June 1996

No one here in the church can comprehend my actions because no one knows my identity. I must go from here because the pilgrim identity must be expressed; for my health's sake and for those yet to be touched by the mission. If I stay, then the identity will remain largely suppressed, not fully taught, and never caught.

The Lord has as promised, provided a good job, a place to stay, and a place to store surplus furniture. The Lord is greatly to be praised. God rarely works with majorities but chooses minorities to fulfill His purposes. I am weak, He is strong; I am incomplete. He is my completer. I cannot seem to be willing to involve my church in the secrets of this mission. I do not want men's voices to muffle out the voice of God. On Sunday morning, I was presented to the congregation as a missionary candidate to be sent out from them, but I am content in myself to go privately anyway.

The day of my entrance into MAGA has arrived. Ten years of preparation, plus eternity past has now seen the Lord bring me through the door. His grace is like a wall; His peace is my comfort. The Central District's volcano, Mount Ruapehu erupted, sending ash over Rotorua City. The sky is dark like judgment. I packed up my possessions into my van and departed Rotorua from the pastor's home at three o'clock. I settled into my cabin at the Murupara Campsite and felt a sense of loneliness creep over me. I cried to the Lord for comfort, and He tenderly sat with me there. I remember that Jesus left His comfort to become poor and alone for me. This refiner's fire is not as hard as some are called to venture through. I give the Lord praise. I entered MAGA with about sixty dollars to my name and with no promised financial support from any church. This is the month of change. The Lord has brought me through a tight door. May He be brought glory and honor to His name and person.

The first days at the superette went well with special grace given to adapt with ease and to be welcomed by the staff. The Lord has kept me in a sweet, joyful, hopeful frame of mind. I know to glow. I have had a supernatural ease to witness to various staff members about the Lord. I was able to testify to two men in the motor camp.

Lisa, one of the superette staff members is also a Christian and a friend of a puritan family in Murupara. I was introduced to this puritan family, and I had dinner with them. Shane and I hit it off immediately as we talked about revival and the state of the Church in this country.

July 1996

God has worked wonderfully in this ministry. The times spent with my puritan friends have been incredibly uplifting. A man who stays in a nearby cabin listened as I told him of a wonderful savior. I am finding that people, strangers, just open themselves like a book to me. I praise the Spirit who is the blessed anointing.

(Extracts from a letter to my peers around the nation)

The Lord's grace has been like a substance; a strong arm to hold on to. I am glad for the prayers of God's people. I am residing in a small cabin at the motor camp at present and I am looking for another place to form as a base of contact with the community. As a pilgrim, I know that the Lord has a mission for me to accomplish as I travel this path. You may hear certain tales about me, but it is important to hear it from the 'horse's mouth.' This is my appointment. I remember how they said, 'What good can come out of Nazareth?' Of a truth, God rarely works with majorities but rather chooses minorities. Further, Joseph dreamed a dream, but in reality, it was God's dream for Joseph. To hear God's dream and to pursue it, is to desire to accomplish your divine mission. With lowly small beginnings, the dream will grow to touch many lives. Jesus, the King of Glory was born in a manger.

Of a truth, the fields are white and wasting, the laborers are few, time is short, and Jesus is coming soon. Why tarry we in the nest as birds with plumage and full bellies? All is decay, strife, discontentment, and idleness. It has been four years and by now the nest stinketh. But rather let us arise and shine and fly and soar to the heights. Let us live the life that we were saved to live.

All glory and praise and honor and adoration be to the King of glory who loved us and washed us from our sins in His own blood and who forever lives to make intercession for us.

July 1996

I was invited to preach both services at another Baptist church on the East side of Rotorua City. The first message was on the theme of open-air evangelism. The second sermon was about the fellowship of His sufferings.

I also went into my old workplace, the supermarket, to see how my converts were faring.

I heard about a flat which is available in Konini Street, Murupara. The landlord's bond was two hundred and thirty dollars. I had nowhere near that figure. So, I prayed to my boss, and He stood up and sent someone who gave me a gift of three hundred dollars. Praise the provider King!

I had dinner with a staff member and was able to converse with her about the Kingdom. She committed herself to Christ. She is the first convert in MAGA. All glory to God who came down to us when we could not get up to Him.

I had an appointment to visit with the new convert. I waited for an hour by her house and the next day learned that she had accepted an invitation to another religious activity.

I have acquired two things lately. One: feelings – God has shared His heart burden with me. I find tears come easily when my heart is touched for my beloved people. And Two: A real hatred for the demons. This is not mere theology, but rather an entrance on to their turf to experience their intense interference to thwart the work of God. This is not a game: this is warfare.

August 1996

I moved out of the motor camp into the flat on Konini Street. The lounge and bedroom are all in one large room. Everything fits in nicely and I have made myself at home.

On Sunday night, I met up with my disciple Marcus again. I still hope that he will be a part of the pilgrim band. During the week I was able to converse with a few people about the Lord.

I am attracted to Lisa (a superette staff member). Every time I attempt to express my feelings for her, the Lord holds my tongue. I guess this is what happens when one surrenders their tongue to the Lord.

Something happened this week concerning Lisa that God has used to sanctify me even more. I have nothing to live for now but the mission. I have become 'kamikaze' for the Kingdom. I seek to be anointed by Spirit. Life is void without that. I am also desiring to join with Eastside B.B. Church folk to street-preach in Rotorua. I would like to accumulate some experience in street work as this is the art in which the band shall be engaged in.

I had a most blessed time with the puritan family at Pohutukawa Street tonight. Shane, Tracey, and I prayed for over an hour together. The Spirit moved awesomely as we prayed for revival, our government, and our nation. We had the liberty to beseech God, claim promises, and yield ourselves as His vessels.

Revival is the theme of our conversations. It burns like a fire in our bones. We encourage each other with stories of saints of old. I sat in wonder at how God had brought us together in this place. We covenanted together to meet weekly to pray for revival in our nation.

September 1996

I am having a bad week with mood swings. I had a great time with Shane as he paced the floor, bound the demons in Christ's name, and called for a healing of the nation.

The managers at the superette are moving on to another position and Lisa is going with them. I am not surprised. Once again, someone whom I adore is leaving my life. The superette managers have invested a lot into training Lisa, and the Kingdom has invested a lot into me. The Lord must have something great in store for the future. Praise God!

An introvertish week for me as I type up the 'Know to Glow' series and 'The Pilgrim's Prayer-life' series.

Shane and I traversed the mount near the northern bridge of Murupara to pray for MAGA and our nation's spiritual health.

On the weekend things returned to that former way in which God operated without my help and organized people to come across my path so that a word in season could be spoken.

I preached at the Eastside B.B. Church with power and passion on subjects close to my heart.

November 1996

My tenth birthday in the Lord was a time of reflection and celebration.

There is activity among my converts both in Rotorua and here in MAGA. I also met with Dennis in the Motor camp and during the attempts to witness to him, there were numerous interruptions, even an electricity cut occurred.

At night I walked to the town centre and prayed for the town, claimed the victory over the demonically controlled assemblies, and asked for the release of their captives.

December 1996

I preached at the Rotorua Eastside Church on the importance of lifting up Christ, for He is the Highest. On Monday, I met with Shane's family and brought the devotion. My health is breaking down because of the difficult workload. I am working a full-time physical job plus the demands of the ministry, and domestic duties.

On Tuesday night, the family from over the road came to ask me questions about the Kingdom. Noelene made a prayer for salvation, and I explained baptism to her. Rex is coming to visit me quite often for fellowship. Mahia is seeking the way. James and Joanne are two teens with good hearts.

On Saturday, Rex and James accompanied me to Rotorua for a men's fellowship meeting. James gave his heart to the Lord. On Sunday night, back in MAGA, James confessed his decision to his family.

In the next few days, there was an interest stirred up with a few others inquiring about this 'new gospel.' Tania and Mahia came over and asked me many questions. Joanne also came and decided for Christ. I am enjoying a revival now. There is liberty, power, and the Spirit's influence.

I held my first cell group meeting in MAGA. James, Joanne, and Noelene were present. We sang songs and I took for my text, John 8:1-12.

We then had supper and a question time. We have also started a weekly games night among us to strengthen our bond.

Every Sunday morning I am transporting inquisitive people from Murupara, in my van, to the Rotorua Eastside Church. James invited his friend, Lucas, who showed interest in the Lord.

The flat next to mine is vacant and I am renting it for cell group meetings with the converts. Now, we can have a place set up for services.

On Sunday, Mahia and his family came with me to the Rotorua Eastside Baptist Church, and Mahia made a profession of faith. I pray to be set free from temporal work to do the eternal work. It is my heart cry. I have been with people every night this week as the Lord draws them. I am as one who is a spectator. He is moving in their lives.

On Thursday night, we had our bible study meeting in the new flat. A few folks from Eastside came and the message was from Colossians 1:12-14. Noelene, James, Joanne, Lucas, Mahia, and Rex were present. We had supper time and continued fellowshipping until after midnight.

Oh God, build your band of pilgrims here in MAGA. Oh, little town of Bethlehem – yet what came out of that place altered the world. I believe that what can come out of this place can affect the nation. The converts are showing interest in being baptized.

January 1997

I preached both services at Eastside B.B. Church. Lucas came forward and gave his life to the Lord.

Certain things have blown up among the converts this week. The demons are here - we run to God, our refuge. We had a good bible study night with two van loads coming from the Rotorua Eastside Church to support the work.

February 1997

What blessed times at the Eastside Church. In the afternoon, we are outside playing volleyball in the pastor's backyard – so hilarious.

I heard about ministers preparing to support me in the ministry.

I was surprised one day to come home to find that my converts had cleaned my flat – what practical Christianity.

This Sunday morning I sang in a quartet in church with Neville, Gavin, and David. The song choice was 'Look and Live.'

Money has always been tight in the MAGA ministry. This week money has come in for ministry needs.

April 1997

My body is telling me to stop; it is burnt out with headaches. Working full time plus travel and the ministry is taking its toll. During this time, the Lord has ministered to me concerning my need to abide. When I entered the mission, I was abiding, and the fruit was evident. Now, I need to re-enter that union.

Rex is interested in the way of the pilgrim. This encourages me. I know that my entering of this mission in MAGA is to recruit laborers for the band. The Spirit testified to this.

May 1997

Rex and I have been spending time together during my week off work. We pray and sing together in the Spirit. One morning we gave out tracts in the street. Rex is getting excited about The Pilgrim Band. I told him that I had long been praying for a band of pilgrims to circuit preach in the nation.

June 1997

I have been anointed and wonderfully enveloped. God has been in my dwelling. He is calling me to give my spiritual exercises to Him to maintain for me. The Master woke me at four o'clock this morning. He raised me up to pray and read the Word. I am enjoying His presence.

I have been summoned to a meeting in Pastor L.'s home to hear that he has to take time out from the ministry because of a situation in his family. The church members are looking to me to provide direction.

The Lord has taken me up in the Spirit to take over the pulpit. The sermons have been perfect for the occasions. The flock is hurting but God is our comforter. We are bewildered but God is our Shepherd.

I have been praying whether it is a good idea to return to live in Rotorua where I can better manage the church affairs and activities. I asked counsel of the Eastside members and got a favorable response. After much agonizing over the case and with assurance, I gave my job resignation at the Murupara superette. This is the Month of Change.

July 1997

This is my last day living in MAGA - the end of this stage in the ministry and the beginning of another. I have cast myself upon my Boss for support in every area of my life. Rex helped me to move into a boarding situation in Rotorua.

I have mixed feelings. Memories flood my soul. Rex is a great blessing. The Lord is surely giving him to me in my great need.

Chapter Four: The Eastside Years

This chapter covers the period of the Pilgrim Preachers third set of five years in the BBC Movement. The shoots are budding as the pilgrim ministry begins to extend its branches to out-lying regions. Read on to see how the man overcomes new challenges...

July 1997

I preached to a crowd in the hall on 'bearing more fruit'. One of the families announced that they will be pulling out of the Eastside Church. Back at my new home, I stood outside in the night and cried by reason of this blow.

On Monday, I went back to MAGA to encourage the converts. Rex has become a dear friend. He makes me laugh in an otherwise serious desert. The Lord has been wonderfully close in the last few weeks as He tenderly leads me through every situation. He counsels me in the stillness of my thoughts. Where would I be without His care and what could I do without His pure Spirit? How good it is to just wait patiently for Him and to be anointed. The world is dead to me, and I count nothing in it to be dear to my soul. There is perfect peace in total surrender and perfect love casts out all fear.

August 1997

Three girls were saved at the bible club this week. What a wonderful salvation for these little ones and what an encouragement for us. I administered the Lord's supper at the mid-week service.

I went to Murupara and ministered to the converts. There is an opening for me to come weekly to bring a bible message. I will send the converts a newsletter every month to encourage them. Rex came back to Rotorua with me to stay for a week. Life is very busy with many things to organize and execute in the church. Every day without fail the Lord sets me chores to do for that day.

I realize that my time living in MAGA was a divine internship. God has done everything He said He would, and I am blessed. This mission is born in His heart and arises for the welfare of my countrymen. God gives His best to those who leave the choice up to Him. He calls me to reckon His authorship, ownership, and leadership of The Pilgrim Band ministry to be so. He says I am Jesus, the master and director of missions. When you give it up to me, then I can display my glory through The Pilgrim Band to release people in this nation, in my way, in my time, for my glory. Today, I acknowledge that the ministry is God's. If the ministry is not of the Lord, then let it fade.

I have no money in my account. Let us see what God can do. I have no other means of support but the Government of my King. Rex and I have personally letter-boxed the village of Kaingaroa with gospel pamphlets. We are also active in gospel tract distribution around the residential streets of Rotorua City.

The Lord has moved someone to give me a financial gift. The Eastside Baptist Church is running smoothly with clubs and activities being blessed by the Lord. Certain brothers came over from Tokoroa to aid me in street ministry outreach in Rotorua.

September 1997

It has been a very busy week in the church. I have felt lacking in spiritual power within, yet people have been captivated by each bible sermon. My mind has been like a drifting anchor concerning my employment. I only have enough finances for this week's board. I wait upon the Lord.

The men of the church have voted to give me a sum of money to secure me for a while. God has provided wonderfully without me having to open my mouth. He always causes me to triumph.

God has been dealing with me lately concerning the ministry. I am hearing voices from both sides concerning how I should employ myself now that Pastor L. has returned to Eastside Church. I am easy whichever way: whether in a manual job or full-time ministry. Every time I open my bible, there is a passage illuminated with reference to the call. I have stood in awe upon holy ground, my eyes have wept, and my heart is burdened for the need.

The Lord preached through me on a Hamilton Street, accompanied by the three men from Tokoroa. I was divorced from public opinion. The Word went out with many gospel tracts, and God was revealed in 'vanity fair'. To me, the experience was beyond words, and I know it to be my future ministry. The harvest is great: is there not a cause to be out where the sinners are? I feel like Moses before the burning bush; like Isaiah before God's throne; like Hudson Taylor at the beach in Brighton. I just want to live in the prayer closet and preach in the street. This means seclusion, loneliness, and death to all that grieves God in me. It is to be a single life, focused upon the world of souls.

October 1997

I met up with Mata and Terry, the Tokoroa men, and we preached the gospel message to the shoppers of Tokoroa. The message brought the claims of Christ to many a conscience.

I also preached the morning service in Rotorua Eastside Church with fullness and sternness. The message centered on the scene of the cross. There was a reality that brought a young woman forward to accept Christ as her savior.

I accompanied a puritan friend called Alan, to attend a conference near the Waikato town of Cambridge, to hear Major Ian Thomas speak on the centrality of the gospel. The messages made an impact on me and gave me a hub for my street messages.

I have no money again, but gifts have come in. God has proved Himself well able to pay wages to His workers.

I heard from my previous supermarket employer concerning a part-time job opening for me in the grocery department. There is nothing too hard for my God. The job being part-time leaves a few days free for the pilgrim ministry.

Pastor L. and I preached in the main street center in Rotorua causing no small stir. God seemed to constrain people to reach out and take a gospel tract. We are reminded that revival cannot occur while we wade in the shadows.

November 1997

God has caused me to intercede for my nation and these local cities. I am working on the publications of 'The Pilgrim Band for Enquirers' and 'The Pilgrim Identity'. These are the days when I am writing up many of my publications.

December 1997

Rex and I spent time with the converts in MAGA. I have been sending them a newsletter every month to encourage them.

The Lord is illuminating the gospel accounts to me and asking me to get to know Him better.

What a year with my God! He visits me afresh tonight to sup. He brought me out of MAGA, the divine internship, and made a way through these months, providing, caring, and counseling. He asked me to prove Him as the God who provides, and it is done. He has refreshed me with the presence of this church family. Praise to Him who is on the throne!

January 1998

Rex and I joined with Mata to preach on a bustling street in Tokoroa. At one point I came around the corner to find Rex preaching. The Word went forth with certain blessings and people were responsive. On Saturday, we went further to the town of Te Awamutu to repeat the act of ministry. Some children were inquisitive as they had never seen the like before. We then desired to go back to Rotorua because I had to preach the Sunday service, but because we were both strangers to that region and without an appropriate map, we got lost and ended up in the Mangakino region. It was nevertheless an education and will put us in good stead for future missions.

Rex and I are both joined as members of The Pilgrim Band ministry. He has come out of MAGA and believes in the cause.

The following Friday, Rex and I went to Turangi, and we had good success talking to people in the street about Jesus. Rex preached in the mall to a small crowd. After lunch, we went to Taupo and gave out gospel tracts to shoppers. We met three boys who showed a keen interest in the things of God, and an English couple who encouraged us in the Lord.

We traveled to Murupara, and on Saturday, visited the converts including my brother in Galatea. I left Rex in Murupara to supervise the converts, while I went back to Rotorua to spend the next few weeks working on my publications.

February 1998

Rex and I went to the coastal town of Whakatane. We ministered on the main street dispensing gospel tracts with good success. Afterward, we spent time with Pastor K. before we retired to the motor camp to repeat the procedure the next day. We encountered many enquiring hearts on this mission.

Pastor C. from Wellington was our guest speaker this Sunday in the Rotorua Eastside Baptist Church services.

Rex and I went to Taupo and in a number of street sessions distributed tracts. There was an initial resistance to the gospel effort and Psalm 106:23 was brought to my mind. A heavy gloomy cloud is over Taupo because of the sins in the place. I received a burden for those under it. A burden is received in the prayer closet and out where the sinners are.

March 1998

My heart is cold because I am willfully lukewarm. I attended a meeting where a speaker from the organization 'Voice of the Martyrs' was outlining persecutions against Christians in certain parts of the world today. His appearance was common, but His speech was with power, and it rocked me out of my complacency. God says, 'Is not my word like a hammer'?

April 1998

The last few Saturdays, certain folks from Eastside Church have been going out to the main shopping complex in Rotorua to dispense gospel tracts and to sing gospel songs. I love harmonizing with David and bringing out the fullness of the song melody to the ears of passers-by.

Last Sunday, I preached about the reasons for open-air evangelism, and that it was good for members to go out onto the streets to share the gospel.

May 1998

We went out to the main shopping complex in Rotorua City with few soldiers but yet many tracts were given out to people, and I was able to preach for a while. We seek to publish the Word, not blatantly offend.

Pastor L's voice is failing him: a re-occurring ailment at present. I have my own thorns in the flesh: sore eyes, headaches, and fatigue.

I journeyed over to the town of Tokoroa to meet Mata for a gospel campaign in the town centre. I felt God's approval and was able to preach, alternating with Mata for lengthy sessions. We departed rejoicing in heart.

The trio (David, Neville, and me), sang in the main shopping complex in Rotorua. We sang soul-winning themed hymns for two hours without any intermission. It was a cold morning, and many hearts were frosted over to the claims of the gospel. Luke 7:31, 32 was brought to my attention. However, one man inquired after the Lord and a few days later received Christ.

I have sought to encourage certain brethren in the region to prepare for the Waikato Mystery Creek Agricultural Field days with a gospel witness. I have personally designed and organized the printing of three thousand gospel tracts for that three-day event.

This period of time has been characterized by open-air, out-reach campaigns to the cities of Taupo, Tokoroa, and Rotorua. I have been accompanied by my pilgrim companions.

June 1998

The annual Agricultural Field Days are on at Mystery Creek, Hamilton. We have prepared for this time for weeks now. The Pilgrim Band has set its face toward this gathering of souls. On the first day, we proceeded to walk around and pass out gospel tracts, while speaking to people. That night, my team lodged at my brother's place just outside of Hamilton City.

On Friday morning, we were caught in the congested traffic heading to the field days, so we turned back and drove to Hamilton Central.

We engaged in street ministry for the morning. In the Afternoon, we entered the field days and proceeded to converse with folks about their souls. At one point, we were standing at the crossroads thronged and pressed on every side by people. We were handing out tracts every which way we could. I realized those words in Matthew 9:35-38 as the multitudes encompassed me. Oh, to have had more laborers standing by my side at that time. Oh, but they could not be found.

That night, we met a fellow puritan, Alan, in Hamilton Central and gave out tracts to crowds that swarmed by. We were just three among so many. We sang gospel songs with the guitar, distributed tracts, and talked to people. We are nothing more than signposts pointing the way home.

Pastor L. brought up a few helpers on Friday and distributed his supply of gospel tracts among the farmers at the fair. Mata and his Tokoroa crew came up on Saturday and during wet weather made some impact in like fashion.

Rex and I returned to Rotorua and gave our report in the church service, rejoicing together concerning all the experiences and accomplishments.

Oh brethren, we must run ahead of the judgment clouds of divine wrath to warn the sinner-man. We must make haste! Come with me, for of a truth, the fields are white and wasting, the laborers are few, time is short, and Jesus is coming soon.

Time is speeding by. Time is short for the sinner-man, who must be saved before the Lord returns. Time is short for me: my time is running out to see my mission accomplished. Time is running out for the church, for the fields are white and wasting. Is there not a cause for us to seek Christ above every other consideration? Is there not a cause to go and preach to warn the sinner-man? Is there not a cause to shake ourselves free from sins and weights which do so easily beset us?

July 1998

Rex moved into Rotorua to reside at my address. We are the best of friends, and he makes me laugh with his extreme love of cleanliness. We are looking forward to continuing our street evangelism ministry. Most Saturday mornings, the Eastside Church folk engage in gospel street work on the main shopping streets of Rotorua. I especially note that these mornings are attended with divine power. The hearers are inquisitive; the passersby are interested.

August 1998

Jason, a workmate at the supermarket, received Christ as savior today. He has attended church a few times and heard the gospel. We waited for the 'penny to drop' with him. He saw Jesus standing and waiting to receive him.

September 1998

Rex and I went to the town of Putaruru and handed out about forty tracts on the main street. We arrived in Tokoroa and distributed gospel tracts to a more numerous crowd. The young people were responsive and the Christians we met were encouraging.

Later in the afternoon, Mata and his family met us, and we proceeded to preach the gospel. The Lord preached through me for nearly an hour with great effect. People were always passing by or sitting nearby to listen.

We had dinner at Mata's house before returning to Rotorua.

The Pilgrim Band is (as I see it) in a strait place at present. It feels like we are walking on a high wire. There is no extra cash, so we are relying upon God for each outreach. The car is on the road daily and therefore at risk. The whole operation is delicate. It reminds me that God's work must be done in God's way, with God's supply. We have learned not to make a move until God tells us to go to a target town.

I took Rex to the Baptist Church building on View Road, Rotorua, and on the front lawn of my old abode, I revealed to him the visions that I received in 1995 and 1996. I shared with Rex the incidents concerning the origin of the pilgrim ministry in the hope that it might draw him in tighter to the cause. Rex was excited and blessed God.

October 1998

The church has been praying for weeks for this next outreach. Chris, a member of Eastside Baptist Church, came with us to the Waikato town of Matamata and helped us to distribute gospel literature. Chris was very nervous but soon warmed up to talk to people. By the time we got to the town of Morrinsville, Chris was running ahead of us to talk to folks on the main street.

Our duty is to be out on the street where the sinners are. We are not responsible for how people react to the news. We usually experience about a fifty/fifty reaction to the ministry message.

On Friday, we went out onto the main shopping streets in Hamilton City. We had a limited number of tracts, which the Lord seemed to multiply until the end of our time there. This is indeed 'vanity fair'- people with plans and places to go all of their own making, people in the chase for fashion and popularity. We gave out gospel tracts to flowing crowds, stopping those with whom we could engage in conversation. Many are close to salvation, and we pray God may help them through. This has been a blessed outreach, and we thank the church for praying for the work.

I am teaching a Bible Institute class and also adult Sunday School in the church, and they are both enjoyable activities. I am waiting for funds for the next mission and doing repairs on the car. The Lord supplied the money for the car repairs in various ways. He owns the car and thus provides for its maintenance.

November 1998

The Lord has impressed upon my heart, a circuit trip to Wellington. I have been shown by peace, the spirit's excitement in prayer, and opening doors that this is of Him. Rex and I are praying for this extensive outreach trip to be acted out in mid-January. We are poor, but our God is not poor. I sent out letters to certain comrades to pray for this outreach. The Lord gave me a verse to claim, And He said unto them, When I sent you without purse and script, and shoes, lacked ye anything? And they said, Nothing. Luke 22:35

Rex and I have been having daily devotions to prepare ourselves for the circuit outreach. Funds came in to provide for the local publishing of eight thousand tracts which I designed. We also have money for our journey.

December 1998

David, Rex, and I went over to Tokoroa to witness during the Christmas parade. Mata joined us and the word was preached. God set our faces like flint against the jeers and reproaches. The Spirit overtook me and preached with rapid fire. Many tracts went out and children gazed at this unusual spectacle. Some teenagers were receptive and others walking with their friends made light of it.

I received my diploma in Theology, after so much time and work. I began my Institute training in early 1992. There have been two interruptions: Rebekah's sudden passing and my internship in MAGA.

I finished my credit hours off in an internship in Eastside Baptist Church.

I was led to open my mouth to testify many times this week at work in the supermarket. The word came through me naturally and with conviction.

On Thursday, I drove to Galatea to visit my brother, who opened his heart to ask many questions about spiritual matters. Later, I visited the converts in Murupara. I heard that Tania received Christ as her Savior. Tania was a moral supporter of my ministry in MAGA. I returned with Rex to Rotorua.

On Friday, I was trying to work out when Rex and I should leave for Hamilton. We were on a mission, and I had woken up with flu symptoms. The Lord spoke to me to listen to His voice on when to leave and what to do. Rex and I arrived in Hamilton at noon, and we were out on the busy street at about one o'clock. During the mid-afternoon session, outside the mall, Mata and Terry joined us to street preach. Mata and I exchanged places to preach the message in two different spots: the mall entrance and the main street.

That evening we spent time with my brother before returning to Rotorua.

Rex and I have been having devotions to prepare ourselves for the planned outreach trip in January, where we will go on a circuit mission from Rotorua to Wellington and back up via Napier.

January 1999

The Lord had to remind me that this is His circuit mission and that we must come through many obstacles in the work of reaching lost souls. The car is off the road with a clutch-plate failure. Alan let us know that he will meet us in the city of Wanganui. Alan is a stalwart friend in the ministry with a heart to preserve the true Word in our nation.

The circuit mission began today as we left Rotorua and made our first stop in the town of Turangi. Here, we proceeded to pass out gospel tracts in the town centre. We wrote down the names of people who talked to us so that we could pray for them and follow up with literature. Rex gave a short address in the mall. In the late afternoon, we arrived in Taumarunui and began engaging with shoppers about the gospel. We erected our tent in the motor camp and spent time singing with devotions. The next day, we were out on the main street again until one o'clock, at which time we made our way to Raetihi. This small town was Rex's birthplace.

Later, we arrived in the city of Wanganui and enjoyed fellowship with Alan and his family. On Sunday, we received encouragement while attending the Baptist church with godly hymns and fiery preaching. On Monday morning, we went out on the main street with Alan and dispensed tracts to many folks. I preached for forty minutes and had good conversations with people. We took down some names for follow-up.

We arrived in the Rangitikei town of Marton after lunch and proceeded to repeat the open-air program. Children are very receptive to the message. We arrived in the town of Feilding at about four o'clock, where we set up at the campsite. We had devotion and a Holy Ghost prayer time before going to dinner. The next day, we were on the main street encountering hardness among the people here. I felt in my spirit a spiritual warfare in this place.

We arrived in the Manawatu region's Palmerston North City after lunch and had more success on the streets among the people. The city centre was packed with people and many tracts went out to hands. The Spirit worked through us speaking with effect upon the hearts. The next day, we came back and spent the entire day in a number of open-air evangelistic sessions. I got in a bit of preaching. That evening, we visited Marcus, who is a soldier at Linton Military Base. Marcus is one of my converts from the supermarket job in Rotorua City. We have stayed connected, and he favours my ministry.

On Thursday morning, we arrived in the Horowhenua town of Levin. We went out on to the main street to do our thing. We felt Satan's resistance until we prayed through against him. We drove down to Otaki and then on to Waikanae. Here, we set up the tent at the campsite. It began to rain, and our old tent leaked. We stopped in to visit Rex's dad. The next day, we ministered to people in the main street and mall area of Waikanae. In the afternoon, we left and distributed tracts outside the mall in Paraparaumu City. Drawing on to evening, we had some time out at the beach.

On Saturday, we met with the Baptist church folk in the suburb of Johnsonville, Wellington. Some of these church members supported us on the main street in Johnsonville. We had much-needed encouragement during the weekend. I preached in the church on Sunday evening on 'The Lie.'

On Monday morning, Pastor C. accompanied us to Queens Mall, Lower Hutt, to witness to people there. I was pleased with this spot because people had to wait for the pedestrian lights to change before they could walk off. This provided plenty of time to pass out gospel pamphlets. A number of children stopped and inquired about the Lord.

On Tuesday morning, Rex and I departed for the town of Carterton and repeated the procedure there. I had a few nasty receptions and got quite disgruntled. In Masterton, we took down many names for follow-up as the Spirit stirred people's hearts.

In Dannevirke (on Wednesday), we met with resistance, but after praying through, many tracts went out to people. The heat and strain are beginning to get to us. We arrived in the Hawkes Bay City of Hastings about mid-afternoon and engaged on the main street with the same program. We have confidence that the Lord will prosper His Word as it goes forth. We have been having devotions morning and evening and it has helped to keep us focused on others and not our own weariness.

The next day, we ministered in Hastings again. While Rex gave out tracts, I spoke bible verses with authority. Passers-by saw and heard the Word. After lunch, we drove down the road to the coastal city of Napier where many tracts went out and names were taken down for follow-up. The Holy Ghost was very sober in me as I spoke bible verses and the people heard the message with power. We rested for a while before resuming with the same manner and effect upon the crowds passing by.

On Friday, we testified in the Napier city centre again. About noon, we left for Taupo, where Rex was keen to go on to the main street. I was weary as the only driver for the whole trip, so I was a bit slow at joining him, but once out there we gave out many gospel tracts.

We arrived back safe and sound in Rotorua to a welcome rest, praising God and giving testimony about all that had happened on the trip. God has made the Christian life to be an adventure.

I have posted gospel material to many folks we encountered on our circuit outreach trip. The church is praying for them for salvation.

February 1999

Rex and I have been out on the streets in Rotorua during this period, being aided by the three men from Tokoroa and folks from Eastside

Baptist Church. We also went to visit the converts in Murupara to encourage them.

March 1999

We have not been out of town all month due to finances and struggles. Instead, we have concentrated on gospel witness in the city of Rotorua. At home, I am recording many of my works on cassette tape because my eyes are weaker, and I can no longer read with ease.

April 1999

Over the weekend, Rex and I drove up to Hamilton and enjoyed a number of sessions of open-air street ministry. I was joyful as I gave out gospel leaflets, and the people noticed it. We lodged overnight with my brother and encouraged each other in the Lord. I am returned to seek the anointing in my life again.

I have been active in singing many songs in the Eastside Church services during this period.

Pastor L. brought a milestone message speaking about how some in the church had taken the 'Christ-life' teaching to an extreme so that they were spiritual zombies who would not act unless struck by a thunderbolt sign. I was relieved because this extreme thinking had pulled the rug from under the feet of some members. When I was keen to march onto the streets on Saturday morning, I would encounter hesitation from certain brethren who would say that the Lord did not inspire them to join with me. During the Eastside years, this extreme philosophy accomplished a subtle erosion even in my soul.

These days are characterized by the same patterns as have long been practiced, namely - outreach in Rotorua, preaching and singing in the church, and encouraging the converts in Murupara.

July 1999

I have a renewed burden to get going through the cities of this land, to take the gospel message to the people. I have a burden to fulfill my personal mission in life which is to run ahead of the judgment clouds of divine wrath.

Rex, Chris and I went on a mission to testify in the towns of Putaruru and Tirau. We letter-boxed these towns in one day. What a strain being all on foot! It threatened to rain, but we prayed for the Lord to hold off the rain. There was discomfort both emotional and physical, but we got there in the end and returned home.

August 1999

Pastor C. from the Baptist Church in Wellington City has asked me to look after his church, while his family visits their Philippine homeland. Rex and I arrived and settled into the pastor's house in the suburb of Newlands.

October 1999

The weeks in Wellington were characterized by preaching three times a week, ministry, and evangelism in the many suburbs of Wellington. It was here in Lambton Quay (a mile stretch of shopping experience), that I was struck with the torrent of souls passing by and it soon became a place of the ultimate outreach experience. We easily exhausted our bags of gospel pamphlets. The Lord prospered intercession in me, so I believe much good was done. The reactions were mixed: some people were hard, and some were eager to take a tract. The message went forth powerfully pleading with people to consider the lapsing time in their lives before they go out into eternity.

It was good to be accompanied by a few Newlands Church members out on the streets. They passed out tracts while I focused on preaching and singing. On the street, the worker can be met with antagonism, so it is good to have support from people of like mind. Further, it was refreshing to meet other street workers (Open Brethren) in Wellington central, who were doing the same open-air ministry work on a regular basis.

November 1999

Back in Rotorua, I had a lousy week at work in the supermarket. Rex is going through a few struggles at present and is on a break in Auckland. Provision came in for the ministry, so I took Danny, (a young man in Eastside Church), with me to do outreach in Tauranga. I felt no divine help to preach, so I conversed with people on the street.

It is my 13th birthday in the Lord. I praise the Lord for giving me these wonderful years in His presence!

Pastor L. has been talking to me about my pilgrim ministry being financially supported by Eastside Baptist church. Also, Pastor C. in Wellington has notified me of his church's desire to financially support me to be full-time.

I have been recording my works on cassette tapes, partly because of my deterioration in health, and because it will help keep me on track for the future ministry. Going over the past helps me to see the whole picture and to see where loose ends fit in together. The Pilgrim Band is my life and reason for living. I must pursue it with all my heart in the remaining time that I have left.

From my awakening years, I struggled with the fact of not fitting in to the church norm. Who was I and what was my place? I knew that I was called to preach, yet not to be a pastor staying in one church for life. Where did I fit in? The messages that indoctrinated me gave me no satisfying outlet for relief. The pastors expected obedience to their leadership, yet I was moved in an independent manner. Refreshing inspiration only found delight in the liberty of being led by the Holy Spirit. There were many struggles over the years. So, where did I fit in? I have never felt inclined to have a family and a mortgage. To be a 'nine to five' Christian has been repugnant to me. I dreamed of an adventurous Christian life.

Only in this last year have I begun to understand something of my place in the Kingdom. I look back and see the thread of The Pilgrim Band Ministry running through it all well before the ministry became an official organization. The Pilgrim Band came out of MAGA as a fulfillment of God's promise to me. Rex and others were added to get the ministry off the ground. I see where I am supposed to be and what I am to do with my life. A good feeling attends this realization. God has led His servant in the right way. It has been a hard and hurtful road for me and my friends in the churches, but the rewards are coming through and I hope will continue to come in the future.

December 1999

A number of people have become Christians in the last few weeks.

Before Christmas, certain of us men from Eastside Church went out to sing Christmas Carols near the city mall, with effect. We were noticed by a local newspaper reporter. This is an ideal time to conduct street ministry because people are geared to the religious theme.

This is the last day of the old Millennium. I remember when I was at college, hoping to stay alive to see the new century come in. Well, here I am by the grace of God. Thanks to the Lord!

January 2000

This is the first day of the new millennium. Wow! I have spent the day in thanksgiving and spiritual exercises. Celebrations from around the world are also being broad cast on Television.

I went on a mission to the Waikato town of Matamata and letter-boxed a few suburbs with gospel tracts. Later, as I lay in the tent at the campsite, I experienced an assurance that this is truly the way I want to spend my days: as a pilgrim preacher.

The Baptist Church in Newlands, Wellington, has voted to support my pilgrim ministry one hundred dollars a week. In addition, they will supply gospel pamphlets for the outreach ministry.

Rex and I went on a mission to the town of Te Aroha, where we conversed with a few people but concentrated on a letterbox drop of the town. The Lord prospered us to finish the whole town on foot in two days. Te Aroha means the love gift. They received the love gift message.

The Eastside Baptist Church voted to take on my pilgrim ministry for fifty dollars a week, plus the supply of gospel tracts.

Rex and I went to Ohakune and Raetihi and letter-boxed those towns. It was a year ago that we had passed through here on our circuit outreach trip, and now we have returned to complete the work. We spent the night in the city of Taupo and ministered on the main street the next morning. This is the first time that I have used an open briefcase on the pavement to display pamphlets and small posters portraying the gospel message.

The ministry went up to place gospel leaflets in letterboxes around a few suburbs in Hamilton, including Temple View – Mormon territory. Later, we were able to converse with two boys at the campsite, who made a profession for Christ. I told them that I would keep in touch by correspondence. On Saturday, we ministered on the main street with open briefcase, tracts, and preaching. The response was good with people willing to hear the message.

Back at home in Rotorua, I was able to type up my first report for the supporting churches. I also typed up a few letters addressing social evils, which are to be sent out to establishments of disrepute.

February 2000

We went on an outreach trip to the city of Tauranga. The Spirit was with me in truth and enabled the gospel to go forth with effect. I perceive the supporting churches were backing this pilgrim ministry in prayer power. There was an emphasis on the blood of Christ during these open-air sessions, and just as well because we had Hare Krishna dancers passing by on the busy street. I felt a spiritual pressure against me as they did their chant and dance. My only relief was to sing loudly, what can wash away your sin? Nothing but the blood of Jesus!

Many people took gospel tracts: this city has a strong Christian heritage.

On our return home to Rotorua, we were able to converse with a number of people and drop tracts off in small settlements along the highway.

Back at home, I compiled a songbook for the street ministry, posted social evil letters to places of disrepute, and letters to recent contacts from the mission trips. God is a continual burning fire of zeal to win the lost at any cost.

On an outreach to the town of Whakatane, we engaged in the usual method of open briefcase, singing, preaching, and tract distribution in the main street. The next day, we returned to minister in the same spot again but were soon told to move on – so we set up in a less travelled patch, We still had a good session. Before departing the town, we met with Pastor K. who is always an encouragement to me. Pastor K. was the man who baptized me in a Rotorua creek way back in the year 1987.

March 2000

I went up to Hamilton City and letter-boxed a few streets. Life in the Spirit is good. Everything is perfectly timed. Burdens belong to the Government of God to take care of. Where God leads there is the provision, power, and pleasing.

April 2000

Last week, I went on an outreach to the small town of Edgecumbe and letter-boxed the town on foot. I was privileged to lead a lad to the Lord.

This week, I went to the town of Paeroa and on foot, placed gospel pamphlets in letterboxes. I completed the town in two and a half days.

May 2000

The Lord spoke to me about proceeding with this week's outreach mission to Mangakino even though the weather had turned nasty. I worked under an umbrella for most of the campaign and finished the village in the late afternoon. On my return home, I stopped off at Whakamaru village and gave them the gospel message via the mailboxes. I was tired but happy.

I sent off more social evil letters to liquor outlets in the Bay of Plenty region.

Pastor C. in Newlands, Wellington, has given me another invitation to come in December/January to look after the Newlands Church, while he goes overseas to the Philippines on holiday.

Tonight, revealed in the stillness of the evening: instead of asking for time off work, I am to resign from the supermarket and go into full-time ministry, embarking from Wellington in January and basing myself in the Manawatu region.

In a sermon, I revealed the new revelation to the Eastside Church congregation and emphasized that I still have to see it confirmed.

Rex and I went on an outreach to the town of Waihi and finished placing gospel tracts in mailboxes in two days. These legs of mine might not look like much, but they have walked the distance. What others despise; God can use for His Kingdom work. We returned to Rotorua and soaked achy muscles in a spa pool.

June 2000

In the last few weeks, Rex and I have been down to Wellington City to preach in the church services. We also travelled to Murupara to encourage the converts and we went on a mission to the coastal town of Opotiki. We run as never sure to run again to bring the message to these souls. The grace of God which brings salvation has appeared to these souls. We returned home joyful in the Lord. May God add a blessing to His Word to awaken sinners and saints to their great need of the Lord, for truly, time is short, and Jesus is coming soon.

July 2000

I swapped my car for a van, with a brother in the church. I will begin to renovate the van into a campervan over the next few months. Soon, I shall leave Rotorua and go to engage in full-time ministry in the North Island.

Rex and I travelled to the seaside town of Raglan on the weekend. The Lord prospered our dispensing of gospel literature in every way, and it was done by Saturday afternoon. Rex lost his beanie hat, and with dismay, we were turning the van around to back track up the street, when we spotted the hat on the grass verge. We were jubilant as no time was lost from our mission.

Wet weather delayed the mission to the town of Thames this weekend, but in prayer, it was purposed to go ahead anyway, and I found that the sky opened on the other side of the Mamaku ranges. I saw the deceitfulness of wet weather – things that look bad but turn out good. The word of God tells us to walk by faith, not by sight.

On the way to Thames, I letter-boxed the small villages leading up to the town itself. In Kope, I discovered the deceitfulness of green grass: the rear tires of the van became stuck fast in mud on the roadside - things that look good but turn out bad. I enlisted aid and was towed out of the predicament.

In Thames, I began letterboxing the hillside town. That evening, I had lonely pangs, being without Rex, but I consoled myself by listening to testimonies on cassette tape and in prayer. When lonely, I can find relief.

The next day, I slowly moved south through the town, experiencing hip and foot pain. The Lord and I had sweet communion there on those hills: our hearts beat as one for the unredeemed populace. Rain showers would come and go, and I would shelter under my umbrella.

Here, I see the deceitfulness of old steeples: they loom high in the town center – fine historical buildings, yet dens of deceit, caverns of Cain, in trappings of tradition.

The firemen were in the park practicing fire drills: I pray that the churches would be as efficient in volunteering and saving souls from the burning.

On Monday and Tuesday, I continued and finished dispensing gospel literature in the town of Thames. This has been an expensive mission: the bank account has been exhausted. God showed me Luke 11:29-32. I may stand up in the judgment and say that no expense was spared to bring you people the invitation call.

September 2000

Rex and I, in the last few weeks, have accomplished evangelistic missions in the city of Hamilton, and the towns of Matamata and Whakatane.

I have just returned from a mission in the town of Te Kuiti. It was the first time that I slept in my van in a motor camp (although the van's interior is not completed yet).

God is slowly gaining ground in my heart as I see the world as Nimrod's Babylon. I am a child of Zion and my King and kingdom I adore. God has been dealing with me about fasting. He is showing me anew to afflict my soul and to seek the God of Heaven. Fasting will help divorce me from the things that I need to leave behind when I venture out into full-time ministry. Oh God, reveal yourself to this nation and powerfully convert the heathen for your name's sake.

October 2000

While on an outreach to the town of Taumarunui, there has been an abundance of rain. The river by the campsite is swollen. I visualize souls in that torrent, swept in its callous grip. Souls are swept by faster than a man can run. Their cries for help pierce the night air. A large bridge crosses the river downstream – the only way to rescue them. Help me, oh God, to see souls saved here in this town! This town is called the 'Heart of the King Country'. May they live up to the name and welcome the King into their hearts. Healing can come to the people of this place but only after the four requirements of 2 Chronicles 7:14 are enacted.

Due to a prior obligation, I had to interrupt my mission to travel in tempestuous weather down to Wellington to preach in the church services. The van was swayed in the gusty wind, but God was in my bark. I sensed a hedge of angels to keep me all the way down to the city. After the evening service, the church kids gave me their financial offering which paid for my petrol expenses.

I travelled back to Taumarunui and placed gospel pamphlets in mailboxes in a few more suburbs. I was not able to complete all of the suburbs in the time period. While traveling to the village of Whakamaru, I ran low on petrol. I was praying for mercies to get me to the next fuel station in time. This led me to contemplate the attitude of sinners to think that they can expect to reach Heaven on an empty tank.

November 2000

Rex and I drove to Murupara to visit the converts. I also went up the look-out hill and prayed – for out of MAGA came forth The Pilgrim Band to be used of God in the nation. Memories flooded my soul; emotions stirred me. I thank my God for my time in this valley.

Image 1: Camp in Turangi

Image 2: Fellow Helpers in Johnsonville

Image 3: On Outreach in Wellington

Chapter Five: The Ministry Years

This chapter covers the period of The Pilgrim Preacher's years in full-time Christian service – the fruit is ripe and bountiful as the ministry travels the width and length of the North Island in the effort to convey the gospel call to the people. These are The Pilgrim Preacher's most powerful years to date.

Read on to see why...

November 2000

Joseph had a dream, but in reality, it was God's dream for Joseph. The dream almost got him killed, but that dream also kept him alive. In the darkest hours, that dream was the only thing that revived him. Many times, my dream has almost brought me to death on the roads. Without the dream, I could just sit and lounge around like many others, but it is the dream that has revitalized my spirit. This ministry is the open door of outlet in an otherwise suppressive camp.

These are the days of setting my face toward Heaven's view. With all my shortcomings and all the evil abounding, I long to enter the pure air of Heaven. I think of that country bought for me by the blood of Christ: the city where nothing shall enter it that defileth or maketh a lie. I am apprehended of Christ for that which I am apprehended of Christ for - I must run my course and fulfill my mission before my departure.

This is my fourteenth birthday in the Lord. Praise the Lord for His wonderful dealings with His servant. Thank you, Father, for coming to save me in Rotorua. You knew I sat in darkness and the shadow of death. Thank you for organizing events so well and for the persuasiveness of your Spirit. For you have delivered my soul from death, my eyes from tears, and my feet from falling. I will walk before the Lord in the land of the living. What shall I render to the Lord for all His benefits toward me? Psalm 116:8, 9, 12

Since I have seen the worldly system more defined as ancient Babylon, I long to be weaned. Soon I will depart, and leave my Eastside church family, my large library, my job security, my home, and my companions. I expect to see God work on me more. I know that I shall have a hundred-fold in Christ.

Tomorrow is my last day of employment at the supermarket. Many things press upon me at present, but the Lord is my refuge: the sweet hour of prayer grants relief. Oh God, keep me on my journey, and may revival winds carry me on to run for the glory of God.

This Sunday morning, after I had preached from Jeremiah chapter one, I was ordained by the laying on of hands to go forth in my ministry. The elders prayed over me and with the sending authority of the church, I was ordained. Now with a single focus, may the mantle rest upon me to see God work mightily.

In the afternoon service, I presented Rex with a certificate of accomplishment for his involvement in the pilgrim ministry for three tours of duty beginning in January 1998.

I went on an evangelistic mission to Otorohanga. At the campsite, I did not feel well: pangs and sorrows came over me. So, I sang, read, and prayed to obtain relief. The next day it drizzled as I walked placing leaflets in letterboxes on the town's hilly slopes. The following day, I letter-boxed the flats by pushbike and was so prospered that I finished the town by mid-afternoon

I returned to Rotorua City, and my last Sunday in the Eastside bible church came and went. On Monday, Rex and I left the city that had been my home for the last fourteen years. We traveled to the town of

Taumarunui. We letter-boxed the suburbs that were left undone on the last recent mission.

On Wednesday, we arrived in Wellington. On Friday, Pastor C. and his family flew out of the country on holiday. While they were away, I pastored the church in Newlands, Wellington.

January 2001

Pastor C. and his family have returned from their overseas holiday. The last month in Wellington has gone well with good church services. Rex has been a good companion in the outreach work. We were able to talk to seeking souls on the bustling streets of key suburbs in Wellington. I have been challenged to memorize and meditate upon scripture more: the key to intimacy with God.

We had our Christian family camp in Silver Stream, Lower Hutt. During the camp, I preached three messages on revival. It was refreshing to meet many new people from regions around the country.

I left Pastor C's house and took up station at the campsite in Porirua. I cried to the Lord in my utter loneliness, and He helped me. The next day, I shared the gospel message in the suburb of Porirua and was able to shine. The Lord gave me this verse: therefore, I endure all things for the elect's sakes that they may also obtain the salvation which is in Christ Jesus with eternal glory. 2 Timothy 2:10

I received many love gifts from the Newlands church family. I spent time with Rex and then took my leave of the brethren to go to the Manawatu city of Palmerston North. I arrived at the campsite about three o'clock and put up the tent. I will use this city as a base to launch out to settlements in these regions. Over the next couple of days, I wandered in the adjacent rose garden seeking relief from emotional agony.

The Lord took me into the city square. I began to witness handing out tracts. The Lord brought along a lady called Marie, who attends a Baptist church in the city. She informed me of the meeting place for the midweek bible study and offered to pick me up that night to take me there. The Lord knows how desperate I am for fellowship at present, so He sent this angel to direct my feet. I met with the church folk that evening and felt better for it. Steve and Marie are a puritan family provided by the Lord to quench my thirst in this wilderness.

I witnessed over the next few days in Palmerston North. There was freedom in the spirit as God did shine through me on the street. I caught up with Marcus (my son in the faith from the supermarket in Rotorua) and met his brother Tony and his friend Chris. We had an enjoyable time of fellowship. Marcus gave me a 'green pushbike.' It was used but it works.

February 2001

I have been active in street ministry and leaflet letterboxing and sometimes I have had assistance from the puritans, Steve and Chris.

Using the city of Palmerston North as my central base, I packed up camp to begin my first outreach trip, departing for Bunnythorpe. After letter-boxing this village, I proceeded on to the town of Feilding and began a campaign there.

The Lord has given me a scripture to claim as I travel from place to place: and, behold, I am with thee, and will keep thee in all places whither thou goest, and will bring thee again into this land; for I will not leave thee until I have done that which I have spoken to thee of.

The Divine Father has approved of the ministry and I am glorious in His eyes. I rejoice at the work that Christ has done in this place. The Spirit has prayed through me for this town. I have experienced a hardness in the hearts of these people when witnessing in the town center, but God shall be exalted above the heathen.

I letter boxed the town of Marton using the green bike, and on the Saturday morning I witnessed in the main street with some effect upon people. Just to be out here is enough, that they may hear and know.

I sojourned in the city of Wanganui for a while, being strengthened with fellowship and sound preaching from the Baptist church. I have been knocking on community doors and also witnessing the gospel on the main street. At the motor camp, lonely pangs have hit me now and then, but the Lord succors me. Steve and Marie (my puritan family) have oft refreshed me – may the Lord reward them abundantly.

March 2001

After leaving Wanganui, I letter-boxed the settlements of Bulls and Sanson. I arrived back in Palmerston North with shouts of joy on Thursday. I re-stacked my van with gospel tracts supplied from the Eastside Baptist church. I sent out social-evil letters to liquor outlets in the region. I spent time in fasting over these matters. Saturday on the crowded main street was a dynamite time of preaching. I had an effective time on the bustling street again on Monday.

The second out-reach tour began on the 13th and finished on the 17th. Using push bikes, my puritan family helped me to letterbox the small town of Ashhurst. On Thursday, I traveled over to the Horowhenua town of Levin and preached in the main shopping street. I am in an incredible position of abiding, with power on my tongue. On Friday, using my green bike, I letter-boxed the small town of Shannon. On Saturday, I letter-boxed the residential homes in the Linton military camp. I have run low on gospel tracts and await the supply from my supporting churches.

I am active in street evangelism in Palmerston North City. At the puritan's family home, I watched a video about circuit preacher, Robert Sheffey. My heart was touched, and I was led into intercession and absolute surrender, which was acknowledged before the Throne. I planned to get away to a quiet place, and God impressed upon my heart to stay at the Ashhurst domain and campsite. I found this place to be the veritable dwelling place of God – this is my Bethel. Surrounded by nature, I can reach out and touch His presence. I feel like Adam walking in the cool of the day and like Jacob rising from his stony pillow. On Tuesday, I spent most of the day praying in the woods.

April 2001

I am house sitting for Ruth, a new friend, in Palmerston North. She gave me a large panel to place under my mattress in the van. Love gifts have arrived from many quarters during this period. While house-sitting for Ruth, I have been able to record many of my works on cassette tape. In contrast to these blessings, my nights have been plagued with dark shadowy fears.

I conducted a follow-up with a man in the Linton village who is anxious about his soul. During a session of testimony on the main street in the city square, Ross, an old friend of Pastor K. sought me out and invited me to visit him in Levin. On Monday, a man prayed the sinner's prayer near the square. We rejoiced together. I encouraged him to attend the local church.

On Tuesday, the third outreach mission began beyond the border mountains.

I letter-boxed Pahiatua and finished the town on Wednesday. Eketahuna was next on the list as I moved south. In Masterton, I stood on the main retail street and testified with gospel songs and boundless joy. Many tracts went out and two came to pray the sinner's prayer. I was also able to converse with three teenage girls about where they were going in life.

On Saturday morning, I preached with some stout words. Later, I visited one of the converts and encouraged him in his church attendance. I then drove to the town of Carterton and letter-boxed a few suburbs before dark. On my green bike, I finished the town on Tuesday and called in to visit a puritan couple whom I had met on the street in Masterton. We encouraged each other in the faith.

On Wednesday, God prospered the leaflet distribution in Greytown, and by three o'clock, I was on my way to Martinborough. God prospered the work here as well and the placing of gospel literature in mailboxes was finished by Thursday evening. On Friday, I was on the bike again in Featherston and finished all of the streets. I was amazed at how quickly I had completed this outreach. I was able to make it to Wellington for church services on Sunday.

May 2001

The last few weeks have been good, but they have put my emotions in a spin and wrung them out to dry. I spent time in Wellington, preaching and door-knocking, and then went to Paraparaumu to spend time in the same activities there. Then I proceeded on to Otaki to engage in witness in this town, where I was able to stay with Chinese friends, James and Alice. The next stop was Levin where I was given hospitality from Ross (the old friend of Pastor K, who had sought me out while in ministry in Palmerston North).

I arrived back in Palmerston North and had dinner with my puritan family. The Lord has laid upon my heart the need to go back up to Rotorua to give a mission report to the Eastside Baptist church. This divine leading was confirmed in two letters which I received shortly after.

The <u>fourth outreach trip</u> began on the 10th, and I letter-boxed the towns of Hunterville, Taihape, Waiouru, and the little villages along the route. Being weary, I was planning to stay in Taupo for the last night, but with a little humor on God's part, He got me to Rotorua in time for dinner at a saint's place.

I preached every service at Eastside Baptist Church for the next three Sundays and was used to encourage the saints with messages exhorting them to stay true to the old-time Christianity of our forefathers. I also brought a similar-themed message to the saints while on a visit to Whakatane. I explained to them a summary of the trends I have witnessed in my travels: many churches are succumbing to the new age plague.

I visited the residential property in Bellingham Crescent, Rotorua, where I was saved, and I thanked the Lord for His kindness to me. I am again set on a clear course to run ahead of the judgment clouds.

June 2001

Back down in Wellington, I spent the weekend with the Newlands church folk, and on Tuesday, I left for Paekakariki, which was consequently letterboxed with gospel tracts. My emotions are held in the heart of the Father as the constant 'up and leave em' lifestyle plays havoc with me. I have missed communion with the Lord. He is the source of everything I have and am seeing done. I am focusing on the Kapiti region during the winter, as it is warmer by the sea, living in my campervan. Life in the campervan is great because God suits me to it, and I am able to use ingenuity to overcome challenges along the way. The Lord makes no mistakes, even giving me a thin build, so as to live in this van.

July 2001

In this <u>fifth outreach period</u>, I have ridden the streets of Raumati, Paraparaumu, Waikanae, and Pukerua Bay.

There was a whole week of rain during this time, but then followed a week of sun. I do not have a flash new bike to use, only this old green bike, and yet the Lord has prospered me so. There have been demonic attacks upon me during this period.

I letterboxed the town of Otaki. Tracts were distributed in the coastal settlements of Tangimoana, Himatangi, Foxton, Waitarere, and Ohau. A great storm came through on the fifteenth of August.

I then proceeded to leaflet drop in the Wellington suburbs of Plimmerton and Mana, and up into the hills north of the bridge. Rex came down to Wellington at this time and we went to the familiar haunts to engage in street evangelism. My supporting churches have given me love gifts which have refreshed me greatly. I am looking to embark on a new mission now that winter is over. The next mission takes the pilgrim ministry over onto the other side of the mountain range.

September 2001

The Hawkes Bay mission, <u>the sixth outreach</u>, began on the 6th whereby the town of Woodville was letterboxed. The larger settlement of Dannevirke was next on the list. God has ordained me a Servant of the Lord to this nation. My make-up, my making, my message, and my means are all testimony to this fact. I preach to people on the street and tell them where they are going in the future.

On occasions, while in street work, my heart has pained me. I know it is frailty. My flesh and my heart faileth: but God is the strength of my heart, and my portion forever, Psalm 73:26. Steve, my puritan friend, gave me a chiropractic adjustment. I had some vertebrae adjusted on my neck and spine that relieved the pressure, giving me relief from headaches that had plagued me for years.

I letter boxed the towns of Waipukurau and Waipawa on my trusty steed, before commencing on to the Hawkes Bay city of Hastings.

During this week, Islamic terrorists struck the Twin Towers site in New York, USA.

My time in the cities of Hastings and Napier was most fruitful with many good talks and souls coming to the Lord on the street. I also met three other groups of street workers in action.

I attended both Bible Baptist churches in this region and was concerned to see the deterioration in them in departing from the sound traditional ways. The next book I am to write by inspiration, 'Chronicle of the Ark', will counter many of these undesirable trends in churches that I have thus far encountered in my travels.

I left Napier and travelled over hard terrain to Wairoa in the East Cape region. I had to stop every now and then to let the old van cool down. I letterboxed the town of Wairoa, and during this time, I bumped into two holidaying members of the Newland's Baptist church, and I had a brief time of fellowship with them.

I travelled to the remote city of Gisborne and spent the next few days in street evangelism. One boy responded to the message and prayed, and I had a good effect on many others. Funds are low and I am praying to the Government of God for relief so that I can organize gospel tracts to be distributed up the East Cape region, while I continue on the road in another direction. I am relying upon the power of prayer alone for this.

October 2001

The money came through and so, I was able to organize the gospel pamphlet drop up the East Cape region to small settlements. I returned to Wairoa and conducted gospel work on the main street. Upon returning to the city of Hastings, I spoke to certain enquirers and preached with immense power on the street. I am enjoying a neat walk with the Lord at present. I am in the habit of fasting one afternoon a week. The Lord is filling in pieces of the jigsaw for me as He confirms my identity as a Servant of the Lord for this nation. A man who knows his identity and his purpose is a great threat to the hordes of hell. I am able to understand more about the 'gained position of abiding' and how that this is the place for His servants to attain to.

I returned to Waipukurau and enjoyed a good time counseling some children on the main retail street concerning the way of salvation. I know my place is to be in the saddle preserving my nation in this manner. So, whether by intercession, writing, or preaching, may God use me.

I came back through the towns to Ashhurst after completing the sixth outreach mission, and stayed with my puritan family for the next few days, being comforted by them. I was given a used laptop computer on which to type up my books. I spent time in evangelism and fellowship with certain of my friends here. I will be leaving for my next mission soon. This is the saddest thing about my ministry: saying goodbye to my beloved brethren.

On Sunday, I attended the Baptist church services in the city of Wanganui. On Monday, I went up from Wanganui and entered the Taranaki outreach mission (the seventh outreach tour). The small settlements of Waverley and Patea were both letterboxed. God helped by holding the rain off and upholding me on the green bike. I retired to the Hawera town motor-camp.

I began the tract drop in Hawera and finished the town a few days later. On the 23rd, Manaia and Normanby received the naked gospel. While there, I received the news that my membership had transferred to the church in Newlands, Wellington. This is the Year of Change and once again I am with a new church family.

I stayed with my comrade Alan for two nights (on his farm near Midhurst), and from here I sent off letters to converts and contacts from the last mission. I have been active in sending off letters to politicians and places of disrepute during my missions. This is one way in which I work to preserve my nation in righteousness.

I began to letterbox the small town of Inglewood but was driven out by rain. I retired to Stratford campsite. Here in Taranaki, we pray that these people would live to see the Lord upon the mountain of His holiness.

As I travel this road, I feel the way narrowing toward the finish line. A pilgrim knows that he has a divine mission to accomplish in his lifespan. My meat is to do the will of Him that sent me and to finish His work. John 4:34

November 2001

For the last few weeks, I have been letterboxing the Taranaki towns of Stratford, Eltham, Inglewood, and Midhurst. The time has been lengthened because of weeks of constant rain. I spent time during the wet days typing up my works, witnessing on the main streets, and attending a church here. Everything I do is for the preservation of my nation. This is my job and my calling.

I received a letter from a lady in Gisborne telling me that she had been saved through my witness. I was able to lead two girls in the sinner's prayer in Midhurst. I prospered in distributing gospel leaflets through the settlements of Kaponga and Opunake.

This is my fifteenth birthday in the Lord. I spent it quietly here in the beachside village of Opunake. I thank the Lord for saving me. Oh, what a mess I would be in if not for the Lord intervening in my life.

In the last few days, I have travelled up through the Taranaki towns towards the city of New Plymouth, leaving the people with a witness they would not get every day. In the city, I walked the main street and passed out gospel tracts to shoppers. After this, I distributed pamphlets through the small settlements of Bell Block and Waitara. I plan to sojourn in Rotorua City over the Christmas period.

December 2001

The Government attempted to pass the banning of smacking policy while the nation is focused on Christmas, but was defeated, thanks to the prayers of God's people.

The Waikato outreach (the eighth-outreach tour), began on the 14th of December. The town of Morrinsville was completed within a few days. I then travelled to Hamilton City and conducted evangelism in the main retail streets over the next few days. Mata and his family from Tokoroa, came up on Saturday and gave me aid in street evangelism. It brought home to me again that if someone of Mata's caliber was with me all the time, then what more could be done? Yea, if there were more pilgrim bands in this nation, then there would be more knowledge of God.

I have been active in recording my sermons and 'Devotion for Motion' messages on cassette tapes. I am also typing up my books and sending off letters to come against social evils in the land.

I letterboxed Huntly and finished the town the next day. We have had a very great amount of rainfall over this period, and yet there is another kind of rain over this country - a more serious threat to human routine and well-being: the judgment clouds of divine wrath are soon to be poured out. Oh, haste to save sinners by directing them to the everlasting shelter.

I letterboxed Taupiri and then Ngaruawahia and completed the town on the last day of the year.

January 2002

I attended summer family camp in Christchurch with folks from various Bible Baptist churches and enjoyed the time immensely. Camp is always a foretaste of Heaven. I met a lady called Beverly, who for the past fifteen years has distributed gospel leaflets in letterboxes all over the south island's rural localities. This is encouraging to me.

Another blessing for me was to be able to street-preach in Cathedral Square (where Ray Comfort preached). A few of us went and gave out tracts around the square and had a great time.

On the 30th, the ninth outreach mission began in Northland, the region above Auckland City. The first place to receive the gospel message was Warkworth and then Wellsford, accompanied by heat exhaustion and heart pangs.

February 2002

I reached Whangarei City and set up in the campsite. I attended the Baptist church here. The mall in this city is a street preacher's dream: it is well set up and people linger and listen. I had great success in speaking to many people here.

On Thursday, I departed and letterboxed the settlements of Hikurangi and Kawakawa. I then proceeded on to Kaikohe, which was letterboxed over two days. The old van motor is prone to overheating, so I could not attempt the arduous roads further north. I will arrange for the postal service to deliver gospel pamphlets to all villages further north. I am praying to the Government of God for extra funds to carry out this purpose.

March 2002

I left the northern town of Kaikohe and completed the settlements of Ohaeawai and Kerikeri. This latter town proved difficult because of heat exhaustion and part of the area being rural. Over the next few days, all the villages on the circuit in the Bay of Islands region were letterboxed. I then returned to the City of Whangarei for a short break.

I rode my green bike to place gospel leaflets in letterboxes in the western town of Dargaville. God prospered me to also cover the small settlements of Ruawai, Paparoa, Maungaturoto, and Waipu Cove.

I am here in the city of Whangarei until funds come through so that I can organize a pamphlet delivery by the postal service in the villages further north. Then I will move on in my journey. I am waiting upon the Government of God. I spent time in open-air witness in Whangarei and letterboxed certain suburbs. I also conducted outreach in the settlement of Ruakaka.

The financial relief came through from one of the supporting churches and I was able to execute the plan for the region.

The tenth outreach mission began covering the South Auckland region. Heaven prospered the distribution of gospel pamphlets so that I was able to complete tract drops to the small towns of Drury, Patumahoe, Waiuku, Tuakau, Bombay, Buckland, and Te Kauwhata. I was glad of good weather and fitness with a divine hedge about me on my travels. I finished the region by giving out tracts on Pukekohe's main street.

April 2002

I delivered gospel tracts in the mailboxes of residential streets all over the large towns of Cambridge and Te Awamutu. I was blessed financially during this period. Chris and Rex came up from Rotorua City to visit, encouraging me in the work. The small settlements of Kihikihi, Pirongia, Ohaupo, and Rukuhia were covered on my green bike.

I travelled up through the Hauraki Plains region, distributing the naked gospel in every village in the circuit. I rested in the town of Thames over the weekend, before the outreach to the Coromandel began.

Blessed is the Lord: for He confirms His word to His servant. He is showing me how my life path all fits together and that His training has been toward a definite end. I know now by revelation, my niche, and I am enjoying my life alone with the Lord in this ministry. I know where I fit into the Kingdom of God, who I am, and what I am supposed to be doing with my life.

I have had the crème of the crop of pastors associated with my pilgrimage. Yet here alone with divinity, my identity has now been made clear to me and I am strong in the Lord and powerful in my God. What I have, I received it from the Government of God.

My God is revealing the next phase of the ministry: that of the 'Jonah method' of street evangelism. This will mean a deeper death as I go toward my own Calvary.

The eleventh outreach mission to the Coromandel and coastal settlements began. God took the pilgrim ministry up the west side of the peninsula, letterboxing the settlements in the bays. Coromandel town was covered on my old green bike. Then Matarangi, Rings Beach, Kuaotuna, and Simpson Beach were done. Whitianga, on the east side of the peninsula, was completed within a few days. It was here that I spoke to leaders of churches concerning apostasy. I am growing a facial beard.

I carried on to Cooks Beach and Hahei. In the coastal town of Tairua, I sat out some stormy weather and waited for more gospel tracts to arrive by courier. After this, the town of Whangamata was letterboxed with great effect.

May 2002

God and I are great friends at present, and He is peeling back compromised areas in my life. I must be single-hearted for the next phase in the ministry. I began the 'Jonah method' in the main street with the old black book in hand.

In the local Baptist church, I spoke to the female pastor about wayward trends.

The twelfth outreach mission to the eastern Bay of Plenty region began in Waihi. The 'Jonah method' was done on the main street in the Waihi township. Waihi Beach was letterboxed over the next few days, and then Katikati. I ran out of pamphlets in the small settlement of Omokoroa.

The supplies came through and with the van loaded with gospel tracts, the town of Te Puke was letterboxed. I completed Omokoroa along with some small settlements along the route heading south.

I organized a shirt with certain bold bible words upon it to be used in the new Jonah phase. The shirt was first used while walking the main retail streets of Tauranga. I walked (as Jonah walked) down the busy street and spoke, giving out tracts while the shirt added a visual aspect. I have such a powerful position of abiding before God's throne at present, having come out of the Coromandel, the power of God. But truly, I am full of power by the spirit of the Lord, and of judgment, and of might, to declare... transgression. Micah 3:8

On my knees before the Throne, I received a premonition concerning interference coming to me from the church hierarchy. I plead with my first love because I dread losing our gained union. At the beginning of the ministry years, I dreaded losing connection with beloved people. Now there has been a paradigm shift, as I dread losing the connection with Jehovah God.

June 2002

The residential strip along Papamoa was completed during the week. As I was travelling away from Maketu, the campervan motor began to splutter. By God's kindness, the van made it to a petrol station repair shop, and the van was repaired by noon the next day. After all the mileage, this old van (though prone to overheating) has never broken down until now.

I proceeded on to the coastal villages of Matata and Thornton. The next stop was the large town of Whakatane. I attended the local Baptist church and had fellowship with Pastor K.

In the next few days, the beach town of Ohope was completed. On Saturday, the Jonah shirt was used on the main street in Whakatane with effect. I spoke bible verses as I walked the main retail street. When one considers that I was a very shy child, this is an amazing feat and testifies to the presence of God working effectually in me.

Next, the town of Kawerau was completed. This ends not only the twelfth outreach mission but also phase one of covering the North Island in this manner. In mid-1995 God commissioned me to run ahead of the judgment clouds. I went into part-time and then full-time ministry, and today, phase one is completed. I rejoice and raise my right arm to the heavens on my green bike. I rejoice in my God and His wonderful works. God has kept me all the way and prospered His servant to finish the phase before winter hits.

The bible promise comes to mind and behold, I am with thee, and will keep thee in all places whither thou goest and will bring thee again into this land; for I will not leave thee, until I have done that which I have spoken to thee of. Genesis 28:15

I have been a vessel through which the Government of God has issued the gospel call to the North Island. I have deliberately spent less time in cities where there is already a puritan gospel witness. Those areas are the responsibility of the churches in them. If I, a feeble man with an old van and an old bike can accomplish this mammoth work, then how about the many folks who sit in churches, and who have mansions and thousands in the bank account?

I thank the Lord, and the people who have supported this ministry. It is a great privilege to be full-time and able to focus completely on the gospel work at hand. And so, whatever I have done day by day, whether letterboxing, preaching, writing, interceding – it has all been for the preservation of this nation in righteousness. This one thing I do – the preservation of this nation.

Image 4: Campervan in Kapiti Coast

Image 5: Camper and Green Bike

Chapter Six: The Darkest Years

This chapter covers the period of living in Wellington, having been asked by the Newlands church to stay with them permanently. These are the Pilgrim Preachers darkest years. The tree is cut down. Read on to see why...

August 2002

During the winter, I spent the time with the church family in Newlands, Wellington. I stayed with Pastor C. and helped in the church activities. In the morning I would type up letters and the book – 'The Pilgrim's Prayer-life.' In the afternoon, I would go out for street ministry in various suburbs of Wellington.

During this period, there was buffeting from the church leadership over the Jonah shirt, the beard, and the social evil letters. Pastor C. indicated that he wanted to divert my financial support elsewhere. The atmosphere became tense, and the pressure increased upon me to stay in Wellington for good and assist in the Newlands Church. There was more than just human influence: there was a darker force working behind the scenes which I could sense.

One Sunday, I succumbed to the intense pressure and indicated that I would stay in Wellington. I could see the needs in the church, and I wanted to appease the situation. I always come from a place of innocence, and I like to please and show loyalty to those who have financed me in the pilgrim ministry.

Yet the desire did not last long – for the next day, I was dying a thousand deaths as the Spirit convicted me inside. That night in bed, God came into my room and admonished me. I trembled and quivered.

Nevertheless, I shaved my beard off as a sign that I am to assist the church in Newlands and give back to these folks after they have now supported me for a period of two years.

I am sad about it because Spirit wanted to use me in the Jonah method from region to region. The Devil fears me in the hands of the omnipotent God. God knows that I would serve Him gladly in whatever capacity or city.

September 2002

I was able to secure a job at McDonalds in Johnsonville, Wellington. I am boarding with a church member until I can get my own accommodation.

October 2002

As I write this, I am in a housing unit in Johnsonville, not too far from the town centre. My work at McDonald's is going well but the pay is poor. I have been under spiritual attack and there is still buffeting from the church leadership. I am teaching adult Sunday School every Sunday morning.

November 2002

I am still having struggles now and then with adjusting to life in Wellington. There is still buffeting from the church hierarchy and at times it greatly disturbs me. I am looking forward to Heaven's view and I do not have a desire to stay down here any longer. The Pilgrim Band is my life and without it there is nothing for me. The pastor has implied that I am independent with my own agenda. He supposes it is because of a foul heart in me, but from my side, I have always sought to obey the Government of God and to finish my mission in life. Right back to the years in Rotorua City until now, this is the reason. I have always tried to do the best for both sides. I am submissive to the same authority that ordains a pastor to shepherd a flock. I have always sought to be led by the Spirit, and in all my travels, this has been so. Now that I have discovered my identity and calling, I do not want to lose it.

I am meeting with a convert once a week to disciple him. He calls me the 'computer bible' because to every question, I produce an answer. May God help me to be a spiritual parent, for this is the time. Spiritual parenthood comes before the departure.

December 2002

Life is not as good as when I was in the saddle. Now I am as any other man. I have lost my position of abiding as a Servant of the Lord and gone is my supremacy over life and man. Some days, I mourn my loss, but I cannot find my way out. It is too late, I think, to try to revert back to the pilgrim ministry. It would be like trying to go against the bible city of Ai. God's plan for me now seems to be to help the church work towards the completion of its mission. Gone are all the burdens and aims. I am just like any other churchgoer. Furthermore, I have no real deep desire for devotion and service anymore. I have no real enthusiasm for the things of God, though I try. Nevertheless, God is my refuge and hope for each day.

In my Christian life, there have been three sections of five years, each helping in a different church. The Lord has divided it thus. At the end of each period, there was staleness between me and the church. This staleness was divine preparation to move me on to a fresh avenue of service in the unfolding plan. In all of this, the mission has cost me much over the years, but with over one million souls reached, it has all been worth it. It has always been my dream that God's people would take to the streets of our nation in the puritan fashion and that pilgrim bands would be a vehicle for staying the hand of judgment.

Thank you, Lord, for leading me and taking care of me all these years. Thank you for the mission which you entrusted to me. It has been my reason for living; it has been my adventure. I remember in flashbacks, the places where we have been together. We must have reached over one million people with the gospel tracts in the seven-year phase.

In the beginning, you impressed upon my heart that I was set for a special mission. You had a special plan for my special life. During the years of unfolding your plan, I remember how you led me along the way and some folks misunderstood my intentions. The plan was not according to the normal BBC mindset. Yes, the plan was designed for a Servant of the Lord. This is why these folks could not or would not see it.

Lord, I remember your gentle premonitions of future places of service, and everything has come to pass as you said. May you train an 'Elisha' to continue the mission to preserve our nation; to reach two million souls with the gospel. May The Pilgrim Band live on as a vehicle to take the gospel message to the streets and to speak to pastors about staying true to the old landmarks. May you raise up a 'Joshua' to take the band into the next stage of service across the 'Jordan river' while I go up the mount.

Thank you, Lord, for keeping the vehicle running, and my travel safe: through much risk, we have come to this side. A hedge has been surrounding me all these years and I have been immortal because you were not finished with me. Through many dangers, toils, and snares I have already come. It was grace that brought me safe this far, and grace shall lead me home. It is a miracle that I am here and able-bodied. I remember so many near misses on the roads. There were dangers while walking the streets, including attacks by dogs and dehydration on the bicycle. I am thankful for the presence of a guardian angel in travel and street ministry.

I remember pushing the bike up steep hills, being divinely taught on my knees in the van, saying hello and goodbye to dear brethren, crying inside, receiving love gifts and giving to missions, waiting on God for supplies, and knowing brethren are praying for me, being held up by wet weather, typing books and recording devotions, leading ones to the Cross and walking in the divine air of 'Bethel'. I recall streets, houses, and places where we were together and bitter-sweet times.

Thank you, Lord, for keeping my health and keeping my countenance full. Thank you for staying with me in the garden where we walked and talked among the roses of the north. Thank you for using me on the streets, in the prayer closet, and in letters to deviating organizations.

Here in Wellington, I am like Gideon in the years after his mission; like Elijah after his return to commission Elisha; like Joseph after the years of famine; like Samson in the prison house; like John the Baptist in Herod's prison, and like Paul who was ready to depart. All these men looked toward Heaven's view.

February 2003

I am setting my house in order, making copies of my books, and distributing them to like-minded friends. I am teaching Minor Prophets in adult Sunday School, and I can impart to the people a more accurate insight into the prophet's makeup.

The 'pilgrim-mobile' failed the road-worthy warrant, and with costly repairs to be done, it has seen its day. So, it was with sorrow that I took my campervan and disposed of it. I will not forget how this van has served me through the miles – this bethel on wheels. It has been my bedroom, office, lounge, dressing room and prayer closet.

March 2003

During the early morning hours I experienced chest pain. God sent His angels to call me so that I would be serious about the covenant between us. Being awakened in my bed, there came an experience upon me in the small light via the hallway. The angels came and there was a powerful lifting up of my soul to leave my body. It was strong upon me and the verse Ecclesiastes 8:8 came to mind. The only thing that kept me from going was my intense pleas, 'not yet, there are things still to do, not yet.' This experience continued for a full minute with my full sight, at a slow pace, with the loud sound in my ears likened to wheels upon wheels.

Now in the morning, I ask God to help me to do what he wants me to do. The Lord is very gracious to His poor servant. He has filled me with fear for He is stronger than I.

April 2003

In McDonalds, there is a saying: 'aces in their places.' This means that when work gets busy, place the best workers in their most efficient stations. I have lost a year; the government of God has lost territory: I have been out of my most efficient station. The politicians are passing ungodly laws. Where are the prophetic voices? What are they doing? They are tied up in several ways, like Samson grinding wheat in circles, blind and bound to some trivial labor. May God use my prophet letters to awaken these ones to who they are and what can be done if they were to get into their most efficient station.

The 'Titanic' ship is going down beneath the waves. Our nation is sinking into the depths of depravity and apostasy. Some church members are hugging within the confines of their cabin, resigned to the death of the nation. Arise, people of God, and stand on deck to testify. There are those who shall soon be beneath the angry waves. Oh God, help puritans to stand on deck to be a voice for thee.

My sweet Lord: free me. Place your hand upon me again and use me. The headman's axe is preferred above staying here in this dungeon. I am operating outside of my gift; outside of my niche: my hands are tied. Last winter was the most disastrous season this country will ever see. I am the Pilgrim Band, and the Pilgrim Band is me. The pastor seeks to dissolve the Pilgrim Band – you damage my soul!

God's people here talk about the issues facing our nation, but they do not do anything practical to address them. In a sense, their job is to raise godly families and support their local church. In a sense, the pastor's job is to feed his flock. That is all good, but just as long as they allow the Servant of the Lord to do his job, exercise his gift, and operate in his niche. They have the freedom to do their job, but then they deny, prohibit, and resist the ministry of the Lord's Servant. This is my grief, and I must bear it for a time. Only God can deliver His Servant and work a new work, that if a man hears of it, his ears shall tingle.

May 2003

Shall I bring to the birth, and not cause to bring forth? saith the LORD: shall I cause to bring forth and shut the womb? saith thy God. Isaiah 66:9

God has been speaking to me every time I read His Word, and the above verse is given to me to claim for my future. The Lord is bringing to the birth. The mother is the Newlands church which must go through labour and discomfort to release the one who has been a burden for the past nine months. The child does not need to do anything: the contractions bring forth the birth. With life there is discomfort, risk, and tears, but also new hope, new freedom, and new joy. Unless there is the birth in new life, there can never be a man child to change the world. The doctor is the Lord, who waits with skillful arms to hold the child immediately as it comes forth. Many contractions are occurring at present. There is pressure in the church, and it is becoming more intense, until soon they shall eject the burden.

My mindset has been to die. I have looked toward Heaven's view. But now there is a new hope. God has been speaking to me again. I am seeking a way out of here in June, the month of change. History is repeating itself in the same vein. There is staleness and a closed man waiting for the revealed way of deliverance. If I stay here, I shall surely die. If I go through the door, I shall die a death to the BBC Movement.

Some of the church folk, influenced by the pastor's untruths, look upon me with disdain. Their countenance is adverse toward me. The Pastor persecutes me subtly from the pulpit on a regular basis. I now know that the health of the 'mother' shall be restored after the birth.

Joseph had a tender heart. He was God's chosen: a special child. God gave him visions of a future mission. He believed in God, and he told his family. They rejected him. They may have responded that it is not the acceptable path. We are your authority; you are not ours. Who are you to declare anything from the Lord?

So, Joseph was bound in spirit. He discovered that he could not freely operate his gift. He found that he could not freely speak of the deep things of the Lord.

Then the story moves on to show how God delivered His Chosen and separated him unto Himself to accomplish the revealed mission. The family ejected the problem and were glad to have done away with him. As the scripture says in another place, Hear the word of the Lord, ye that tremble at His word; Your brethren that hated you, that cast you out for my name's sake, said, Let the Lord be glorified: but He shall appear to your joy, and they shall be ashamed.

And so now, beloved Joseph was divinely separated solely unto His master, to be led by the highest authority: the Government of God.

He heard the voice of God and became a man to stand in the gap for the nation. (He that hath ears to hear let him hear that this path is for about ten percent of God's people).

June 2003

The veil is pulled back: for life is best lived forward and best understood backward. I can see a little clearer about what was going on last winter. One or two people wanted to see better results as in, new people coming into the Newlands Church. Pastor C. wanted to re-direct my financial support, and this unsettled me. Pastor C. did not like the Jonah method, and this upset me. He assumed my travelling ministry was over, and this flummoxed me. Pastor C. had changed in his countenance toward me and pressured me to stay in Newlands. I desired to be loyal to the Newlands Church which had given me so much aid during my ministry years. All these factors were apron strings that influenced me at that time. It was a season in the 'pressure cooker.'

So God concluded to Himself, I will go along with it for a season to divorce him from the Newlands Church and the BBC Movement, to be wholly mine. I will deliver him and bring him to work outside of the nationwide Movement. If he comes out, then I shall provide for him a 'Cherith' for restoration of soul and foundation of ministry.

And again, the Lord has spoken saying, I will set my eyes upon him for good and I will bring him out of captivity to a new place. I will build him again and not pull him down; I will plant him and not pluck him up. I will lose him for a time that I may gain him forever. And I will give him a heart to know me, and he shall be mine: for he shall return to me with his whole heart.

For a small moment have I forsaken thee; but with great mercies will I gather thee. In a little wrath I hid my face from thee for a moment; but with everlasting kindness will I have mercy on thee, saith the Lord thy Redeemer. Isaiah 54:7, 8

So, now I see clearer and that the tight spot here is like the elect before the Red Sea: salvation is of the Lord! They think that for me to go outside the BBC Movement is to lose my crown, when in reality, to go out is to keep my crown. There is intense testing at present, to see if I really want the ministry again. Will I put the ministry over and above comfort, job security, and convenience? God deals with a Servant thus because the stakes are high. The cost has to be high to effect a great change in the nation. The cost has to be abnormal to effect a great change in the Servant. I must return to the place where I had the power to come against the 'Jezebel' in Parliament.

I am not aware of any like man in history who changed the world while having to be under submission to a common pastor's authority during his ministry years. I have been a fool to have remained in Wellington and to have fallen into this trap where Satan is allowed to repeatedly kick me in the gut with the pastor's shoes. If Satan cannot take a Servant out by using the world, then he will use the people of God, and after this, female attraction. Satan fears a Servant in a beard, a shirt, and a secret place. I will repeat those words of the prophet, oh that I had in the wilderness a lodging place of wayfaring men; that I might leave my people and go from them.

September 2003

Over the winter, I tried to get a job in the Manawatu region, but no door of deliverance opened. I have been in Wellington for one year now and this has been a turbulent period. Nevertheless, during this month, I have experienced the blessing of the Lord upon me, and I am excited about the things of God. There is firmness from Spirit that I walk uprightly before Him in order to be a clean vessel to speak to workmates and in the church services.

October 2003

During this period, I have had serious battles with envoys of Satan: spirits sent forth to buffet me. I was once the head, but here I am the tail, and they are missing no opportunity to put the boot in. I am under extreme mental and emotional pressure. There is weekly persecution from the church pulpit. I have confusions of mind, and this is undermining my foundation for life and ministry. This month, I have been trying to discern truth and error and to renounce the enemy from my life. I have experienced spiritual assault, especially at night while in bed: it or they would come and press me into the mattress until my pleading of the Lamb's blood made them depart.

November 2003

I am dead and empty inside. Inspiration is dried up. God seems distant. I want to sit and hide away. I doubt all the things I used to strongly believe in before. I am also looking at other Christians who hold properties and large bank accounts and wonder if the sacrifices I have made are worth it. I am being stamped upon weekly from the church pulpit by the biggest boots one can have and it is taking its toll. Where once I had sensitivity, now I have no tears. I have no fear of God, and no ability to repent. The pastor is the problem because, firstly, his accusations are hardening my resolve to resist his malicious agenda, and secondly, it is useless for me to try to raise myself up again just to be knocked back down.

This is all compounded by the fact that I have no one to confide in; no one I can trust in the church to keep confidence. I bear this alone, and that is why it is taking so long to work through. Even the things I do say in casual conversation to members come up with a mocking bent from the pulpit.

One might wonder why I can't expose the dire situation to people in the church. Well, I will try to explain it like this: first, even as I remain silent there is an agenda to trap me with some evidence to prove that I am a troublemaker. Second, I am at the 'top' of the BBC Movement and I have an excellent reputation which will be trashed by this pastor if given the chance. Third, the BBC Movement holds such immense influence over my head that to be forced out of the Movement seems the height of vulnerability to the dark forces.

February 2004

Every meeting, every week, there are subtle attacks from the pulpit upon the white people in the Newlands Church assembly. The Asian people are left alone. There are innuendos and forms of manipulation confronting us every Sunday. There is an influence working behind the pastor who is possessed with a campaign to rid his church of white church members. This is the pastoral mindset: to purge the church of 'dead wood.' In other words, to get rid of members who are not malleable into clone-hood.

The constant theme in the pastor's sermons for the past eighteen months has been 'unconverted membership.' Sayings from the pulpit have come forth such as unconverted pretenders; troublemakers in the church; faithful Christians attend three services a week, while the unfaithful only one service; and whoever leaves the church is unfaithful to the pastor. Can one imagine what this barrage does to genuine people over the course of eighteen months?

One thing that bewilders me here is that the members of this church say nothing and do not react to the mean-spirited sayings coming from the pulpit on a weekly basis. Intelligent people put aside their reasoning powers when they enter the door and accept anything from the pulpit as from the Spirit.

Is communication with Pastor C. the answer here? I have found out that it is not. To address the issue is then to be monitored, interrogated, and preached at. I am not the only white person in this situation, and I see how the others are mocked and their reaction played down. Some of the white people have already left the church; others will leave in time.

March 2004

In the church building, while fellowshipping after the service, I noticed that the pastor positioned himself to eavesdrop and to try to catch some word from me to bring against me. This is ridiculous! What kind of activity is this? He is desperate to discredit me as a troublemaker. I must leave Wellington City somehow. I do not know how, and I cannot think clearly about it.

I cannot continue here where I am unwanted, demoralized, and unable to blossom. I work best when able to follow inspiration. I need liberty for inspiration to flow to produce my best work. To depart from Wellington is the only way to regain that inspiration in the Lord's work again. But to leave my comrades in the BBC Movement is an arduous thought to me. One of the reasons I stayed in Wellington was because I felt an obligation to pay the Newlands Church back for all the bounty, they had given me during my ministry years. After almost two years, I consider that my time is up here, as I have paid the hierarchy back with my free service.

April 2004

I have been here in Wellington for almost two years and every adult Sunday school series that I have taught has come under some form of ridicule from the pastor. My weekly song-leading efforts are also knocked by Pastor C. Furthermore, when I have asked the pastor for teaching and song-leading aids, he has deliberately procrastinated on acting for months.

I am making arrangements to leave for the Horowhenua region. I have a job interview on Monday morning. I have come to the stage where I will just leave as a career move (not a ministry move). I will go out to the Horowhenua region to have a sabbatical.

I have come under severe demonic attack over the last few nights: heightening fears and doubts about my leaving the Baptist Church. The attacks entail a fierce pressure pushing me into the mattress and a screeching noise heard coming from the spiritual realm.

The apprehension of leaving my church support network to go out alone is playing on my mind. I will be stepping outside the hedge of protection. My mind is going to and fro on this issue. I have fears of being overcome (out there) with vices, regrets, loneliness, and spiritual oppression. My greatest fear is for me to get out there and find that God has abandoned me. Here, I am not able to recover myself - who I am in the kingdom of God - nor do I even wish to try because of the weekly demoralizing attacks from the pulpit.

Thanks to my church friend Alex, The Pilgrim Band's internet site was activated on the 21st of April, showcasing some of the articles I have written on reformation, revival, and evangelistic themes.

May 2004

I talked to Pastor C. about how I was feeling. During the private conversation he seemed distant through the whole time that I was opening up to him. It fell on deaf ears because the next Sunday the assault continued. There was no positive change made from our talk. He will continue to chase a flea on a dead dog as Saul did to David. Oh, pastor, you say in a sermon that there are weeds in your garden. You say that the flowers are all closed up. Check what is in your own Watering Can then. You have been harassing certain members for years.

Late on Sunday, Pastor C. came to visit me in my flat, as I had not attended the evening church service. We talked about things, and I told him how my spirit was deflated. He opened up to me and confessed his dislike for certain brethren in the church. He is tired of being messed about by church members.

This Psalm came to my mind: I said, Lord, be merciful unto me: heal my soul; for I have sinned against thee. Mine enemies speak evil of me, when shall he die, and his name perish? And if he comes to see me, he speaketh vanity: his heart gathereth iniquity to itself; when he goeth abroad, he telleth it. All that hate me whisper together against me: against me do they devise my hurt. An evil disease, say they, cleaveth fast unto him: and now that he lieth he shall rise up no more. Psalm 41:4-8

Over the last few Sundays the pastor's attitude has not changed: it is still dark toward me and certain other members. I do not see how I can stay at all, and I do not have the heart to attend all the church services. At the end of the month, during a Sunday evening service, the pastor announced a newly crafted church constitution that tightened the rules for church workers. Now all who stand behind the pulpit must attend three services a week. This is a new weapon in his arsenal to get me out of the pulpit (and eventually out of the church). While going over the Constitution, he also threatened church disciplinary action against opposers.

There is a Servant of the Lord in Marlborough who was named a troublemaker and put under discipline in the Baptist Church there. Since then, Pastor C. has ached to have the same experience so that he can look like a hard-done-by pastor.

Pastor C. also indicated that he expected people to notify him if they were planning on leaving the church to go elsewhere, but I know that this is just to get more ammunition for attack: especially if you are a white person. Over the course of my time in Wellington, three Asian families made career and location moves and there was little fuss, but when white families left the church, there was mockery from the pulpit.

June 2004

In the first eighteen years of my life, I grew up a natural man on the farm. The second set of eighteen years I spent in the foremost trenches in the BBC Movement. I am thankful for the eighteen years of being blessed by God in His service. Now after these two years in Wellington, I am more mellow and careful in how I treat people. I realize that I have just spent the last two years reaping what I have sown. This is similar to the scripture which says, seventy weeks are determined upon thy people and upon thy holy city, to finish the transgression, and to make an end of sins, and to make reconciliation for iniquity, and to bring in everlasting righteousness, and to seal up the vision and prophecy, and to anoint the most Holy.

Now as the third set of eighteen years is about to begin, let no man trouble me.

Pastor C. has removed me from the church duties of song-leading and adult Sunday school teaching. Pastor C. is happy now. This is what he has worked toward for the past two years. I am now sitting at the back of the church like many puritans in the nation's churches. And yet the astonishing thing is that the people in this church exhibit no reaction to what the pastor has done to me.

Satan could not take me out by using the world, so he has used this means. Satan attacks God's Servants through family, finances, friends, and females. Satan aims to disturb the Servant's faith, fidelity, and future. I have suffered on every count. Now my focus is not so much on the harm done to me, but rather that the pilgrim ministry has to be preserved by my going away into a new set of eighteen years.

July 2004

I don't feel like going to church services because every sermon is a gun aimed at me. Pastor C. demands that we attend every church service, but then he attacks the converted. (This is the B.B. mentality). If he had ceased from pursuing a flea on a dog and had focused on encouraging us, we would all be better off today. In the Sunday morning sermon, he used three Kiwi members to illustrate a negative point. In the evening service, he preached about murmuring and people leaving town, directing it at me. Is there any wonder why I keep my going away from the city private?

August 2004

I was able to visit a Brethren chapel in Levin, Horowhenua, and a member offered me a flat to rent in his complex. Thanks to the Lord. I have also obtained a full-time job in Levin. I moved my furniture up to the flat on the 7th and started work in a factory on the 9th. I gave notice to Newlands Church on the 8th. I went back to the church on the 15th to make my last appearance.

My new life (third set of eighteen years) officially begins today.

O bless our God, ye people, and make the voice of his praise to be heard: Which holdeth our soul in life, and suffereth not our feet to be moved. For thou, O God, hast proved us: thou hast tried us, as silver is tried. Thou broughtest us into the net; thou laidst affliction upon our loins. Thou hast caused men to ride over our heads; we went through fire and through water: but thou broughtest us out into a wealthy place. I will go into thy house with burnt offerings: I will pay thee my vows, Which my lips have uttered, and my mouth hath spoken, when I was in trouble. I will offer unto thee burnt sacrifices of fatlings, with the incense of rams; I will offer bullocks with goats. Come and hear, all ye that fear God, and I will declare what he hath done for my soul. Psalm 66

Chapter Seven: The Hidden Years

This chapter covers the period of my first few years in the Horowhenua region. These are the Pilgrim Preachers sabbatical years where the tree sprouts again. Read on to see how the story concludes, thus far...

October 2004

I am now on the other side of the door. I have been released from the trial in Wellington and after two years of being put down, my feet stand on freedom's soil. I am like Nebuchadnezzar who after eating grass for his folly has returned to the royal palace. I am like Elijah who has returned to the land to engage in his second chance.

I was beset by many fears while still in Wellington about leaving the Church and stepping out of the BBC Movement, but I have found it to be controlled and expedient. I just have to take responsibility for my own walk and keep the water out of my boat and all shall be well.

During the past two months, I have allowed myself to settle into the town of Levin, heal, and recover. The Lord has touched my heart and counselled me over a few things. I know what Moses felt like before the burning bush: lost confidence, damaged faith, and comfort zone warmth.

In the past, pastors limited me, broke my zeal, and steered me in their direction. Now, I have no such restraints. I am free as a Servant of the Lord to run for the Government of God. I can go letterboxing again. I can go street preaching again. I can come against the devil residing over the Parliament. I can be that man again.

I want to record my works for prosperity and the preservation of the nation. Inspiration has long been trampled. Wellington was a time when I was enclosed and suffocated. Like wild and free John the

Baptist, confined within Herod's walls, I could not make noise, shout and let it out. It was claustrophobic inside the Wellington hills. The flat unit in Johnsonville was a concrete box with paper-thin walls. I was thronged about with crowds, and I could not make a noise. I had to get out to a beach to roar into the waves and send my perplexity upon the winds. This is why Levin means so much to me. The Horowhenua region is flat, expansive, and symbolizes freedom.

November 2004

This morning I went out before the Brethren church service began and letter boxed up the street. It felt good to be in the old practice again. God is teaching me in the book of Isaiah. I thank Him for His restoring grace!

Thank you, Lord, for your preservation upon me and your provision with a wonderful place to rest my head. I have a computer for my ministry and a web site to display my publications. I have begun advertising the website in newspapers. I am arranging for social evil letters to go out nationwide.

It has taken me over a decade to discover who I am, where I fit into the Kingdom, and what I am supposed to be doing. I had better make sure that I am the best Servant of the Lord that I can be. I need to return to the man who had fire, thirst, initiative, intercession, and a pilgrim mindset.

At present in a manual job again, I am living below par. I am dejected because of the demoralizing years in Wellington. I am not in a place to attempt any substantial witness program. God is counselling me to draw closer into His presence. Is there not a cause that I be in the gap for the land again, especially when the nation's government is marching forcefully on its secular pathway? But to have power with God, one must be single-hearted. I am far from this state at present.

December 2004

Yesterday, I purchased a new bike and fitted it with accessories from the old green bike. I went out and letterboxed just like old times. I rejoiced in my sweet Lord. I smelt the fragrances in the air, and it brought back memories. I rode well, slipping gospel tracts in slits just like in the old days. Thanks be to God for this gift to His servant.

I spent Christmas day with my puritan family and the following day in their church. The spirit in me is jumping for joy like some 'jack in the box' long suppressed, suddenly freed. I also visited 'my bethel' in the Ashhurst Domain and received a blessing. I feel the moving of the Spirit again, which I have not felt since the middle of that dreadful winter when I was knocked out of the saddle. Now like a tree, God is beginning to cause me to bud again, hopefully to return to my former glory.

January 2005

I have divided the Horowhenua town of Levin up into four segments and have just finished letter-boxing segment one. I am excited about doing the work and looking forward to a new year of opportunity. May God preserve me so that I can work to preserve the nation.

The two periods in my Christian life that have been the most damaging to me, my ministry, and my nation are the two main times that I have listened to elders in the church asking me to come and settle and help them. The first time was when I left MAGA to help in the Eastside Church, Rotorua, in the pastor's absence. I was damaged by certain brethren who pushed an extreme Christ-life philosophy which corroded my rationale. The second time was when I came out of the Coromandel region as the Power of God and had to winter in Newlands, Wellington. Certain men interfered with my course and influenced me to settle in Wellington. Both I and the ministry went down into the mud under the biggest boots.

Now in my new town I have decided to keep a reasonable distance from any B.B. Church. I can run faster without the time-consuming interference, but I do miss my people. The pangs of heartache are deep felt at times. I feel lonely outside the BBC camp. Nevertheless, the folks in the Brethren Church here are supportive and refreshing.

August 2005

Having been recently connected to the Internet, I am able to download a few software programs to record my original songs and publish my books. I am busy preserving my inspired works.

December 2005

I have been under satanic attack during this period. I have experienced forms of interference. There have been disturbances in the night seasons. Like Paul, I have a demonic agent to buffet me, who has followed me in my travels.

April 2006

Typical of BBC folk, I sense that if not for my free gifts, some of my fellow Baptist comrades would completely cut me off. I have stood with these men, excelled them, and yet they are ready to cut me off. One realization that has appalled me is that no saint from Rotorua city has come to seek me out, sit down with me, put their arm about me, and say that they want to hear my story.

Furthermore, there is a change-over, in that while my comrades were raking thousands into their bank accounts, I was a front-line soldier up to my knees in mud in the trenches with only an average of three hundred dollars in my bank account at any given time. Now, I am prospering and certain comrades (including my brother), are upset about it as they sink into their freshly dug foxholes.

May 2006

I purchased a laptop computer and a new acoustic guitar to aid me in the ministry.

Concerning my job in the factory, my shift hours have been changed to the evening – this frees me up to do my projects in the morning when I am freshest.

June 2006

I would like to record a summary of my heath journey. As I have recorded in previous entries, I have been suffering for years with pressure in the head, sore eyes and headaches, to the stage where I could not even read a page. I also suffered from fatigue and dizziness if I worked extreme hours. I spoke to my puritan family in the town of Ashhurst about this and Steve (being a chiropractor), adjusted me over a few sessions and relieved my tension.

Recently, I have been receiving therapeutic massages and it is making a great difference to my health status. This massage therapy is effective on relieving the tension in my entire body. Now I understand the way the body is connected – if my sacrum goes out of alignment, the tension travels up my spine and causes compression.

I record this because I am not alone in this affliction. Some people can be too spiritually minded to benefit themselves with any physical good. I went on for too long suffering in silence for the Kingdom.

September 2006

I have been spending these last few weeks in an outreach trip, updating the pilgrimband website, and editing my audio recordings.

October 2006

I have been converting certain publications of mine into web pages on the ministry website. I have also set up classified advertisements for the pilgrim ministry website in many newspapers around the country. I have also been working on producing The Pilgrim Band's debut album – 'All in Good Time.' This album features many of my original songs and a few familiar hymns.

December 2006

I have finished the Debut album 'All in Good Time'. The pilgrimband website has had a colour scheme revamp.

I have suffered attacks from the dark enemy this month, some in the workplace and some in the night seasons.

January 2007

The Lord has been opening my eyes to what the bible actually teaches on a few important issues. I rejoice under the smile of the Lord that He has shown me these things: the scriptures all fall into place without any wresting.

I have begun to type up my Memoir, taken from extracts in my journals. I have also begun the second album – 'Street Songs.' This album features many of the songs I have sung on the nation's retail streets during my ministry years.

My health journey has taken a good turn after a visit to a naturopath, who gave me advice concerning diet and detox methods. The changes to my diet have been incredible. I have exchanged convenient processed meals with fresh vegetables. I have also reduced soy and gluten from my diet. The effect is a clearer head and a better release of toxins from my body. I regularly practice stretching exercises to further aid the body's balance.

March 2007

I registered an account with another website hosting firm to design a site to host my e-books and bible study series.

October 2007

I have been compiling and uploading my publications in E-Book format to the new site.

December 2007

Well, this year is almost over. I am ready to go on holiday in Rotorua City. This time away will be my 'roots tour' as I re-visit buildings, streets, and parks which hold memories for me. I want to survey the family farm and my old schools. I want to complete a long-desired goal – to walk where I once walked and to touch the soil which is the ground and foundation of who I am, and what I have accomplished. What I mean is that if I can conclude the past, then I can rest in the present, and stretch myself toward the future in this ongoing dream.

Every event is governed by numbers: the timing of birth, events, and one's death. I will share an insight into my extraordinary journey.

In my Christian life, there have been three sections of five years, each helping in a different church. The Lord has divided it thus. At the end of each period, there was staleness between me and the church. This staleness was divine preparation to move me on to a fresh avenue of service in the unfolding plan. Every five years I was divinely moved on to another church; another fresh field of service.

Eighteen is another number that features in my pilgrimage. I was brought up in a nominally religious home that was moral, ethical, and grounded. I was raised on a farm and as a result, was close to nature daily. This was my lot for the first eighteen years of my life of which the focus was <u>Family</u>.

After I left the family home and moved to Rotorua City, I joined a fundamental church group and became earnest about this acute belief system during the second set of eighteen years of which the focus was <u>Church</u>. This book focuses on that period.

Now, in the third set of eighteen years of which the focus is the <u>Arts</u>, I have evolved within myself, graduating into this present belief system of higher understanding and expression.

I testify that when I came to live in the town of Levin, that this was more than a chapter change. The <u>part</u> changed; the focus changed; the energy changed, and the allegiance changed.

Conclusion and Glossary of Terms

Dear reader. Thank you for your interest in the story of The Pilgrim Preacher. You have picked up many nuggets during this story of the pilgrimage, but here I felt that I need to list a few main points of conclusion:

1: The story is about a man battling through programming and wills of men to discover his true identity, calling and niche in the kingdom of God and then to pursue that path to its fulfillment.

2: The story emphasizes the reality of the power that can be displayed through a man who knows his niche in the kingdom of God.

3: The story reveals the development of The Pilgrim Band Ministry and the work of preserving the nation in righteousness.

4: There is a reality to the intimacy between the man and his God from the day of salvation to this date, which is the source of the power for life and service.

5: The local church is a hot-house for speedy growth and refreshing fellowship, under the ministry of a man of God in the pulpit.

6: God gives a divine dream to each of us and we must pursue it against all odds as we co-operate with God to see it fulfilled in our lives.

7: God can use Memoir of a Pilgrim Preacher to draw you closer to His bosom and fulfill all of His good purposes in your own life.

In the memoir I have not used surnames of friends, family or pastors so as to avoid any breach of trust and privacy with these people. I come from a place of innocence. I have carefully considered how people are identified in this publication and have no intention to cause offence to anyone mentioned.

Below is a **glossary** to aid the reader with clarification of certain abbreviations and key relationships found in the entries.

BBC – Bible Baptist Church (There is a nation-wide Movement).

M.A.G.A. – Murupara and Galatea Area.

Overseas trip – my trip to Indonesia and the Philippines during the Awakening years.

Pilgrim – a sojourner/one who journeys to a sacred place, physically and/or spiritually.

Field-days – an annual agricultural fair held near Hamilton City.

Puritan family – a conservative Christian family in the area who take me under their wing.

Marcus – a convert and son in the Faith from the supermarket in Rotorua.

Rex – a friend and colleague who helped in The Pilgrim Band Ministry.

Mata – a friend and colleague who helped in The Pilgrim Band Ministry.

Alan - a friend and colleague who helped me in street evangelism.

Pastor O – an American pastor/my spiritual parent during the Early years.

Pastor K – a national pastor who baptized me and encouraged me.

Pastor W – a national pastor who trained me during the Awakening years.

Pastor L – a national pastor who ordained me during the Eastside years.

Pastor C – an Asian pastor who supported me during my Ministry years.

Letter boxed - hand-delivered gospel pamphlets in residential mailboxes.

<u>Book Note:</u> A Bold type beginning a paragraph indicates a new journal entry.

Don't miss out!

Visit the website below and you can sign up to receive emails whenever Pilgrim Preacher publishes a new book. There's no charge and no obligation.

https://books2read.com/r/B-A-YRSZ-BYUQC

BOOKS 2 READ

Connecting independent readers to independent writers.

Also by Pilgrim Preacher

Watch for more at www.xcelbiblestudies.weebly.com.

About the Author

In John Bunyan's famous book, Pilgrim's Progress, the main character, Pilgrim, came from the City of Destruction, and he journeyed to the Cross, and then he traveled on that narrow path toward the Celestial City. This book inspired The Pilgrim Preacher to walk the path of a pilgrim and to go beyond both in spiritual depth and in adventures. Drawing from his deep understanding of the scriptures, he has written many e-books on scriptural themes that will help us in our journey toward that Celestial City.

Ordained with over thirty-five years of theological experience and having e-books distributed in online bookstores, The Pilgrim Preacher is your one-stop shop for sermons and bible lessons.

In this series, the e-books can be used in various ways: as devotionals; to memorize scripture; as guidebooks; and as a catalyst of inspiration.

Buy each book in this series to be the best you can be.

Read more at www.xcelbiblestudies.weebly.com.

About the Publisher

The Pilgrim Preacher in conjunction with <u>Xcel Bible Studies</u> publishes original **Bible sermons, lessons, and devotions** to support clergy and teachers in delivering formatted, tested, and ready-to-go messages on revival, evangelism, and Christian assurance.

http://www.xcelbiblestudies.weebly.com

These sermon outlines are essential for use in bible conferences, family bible camps, mid-week bible study, one-on-one discipleship, bible college block courses, adult classes, personal bible study, and more...